PREPARING MY HEART FOR

MOTHERHOOD

Books in the **Preparing My Heart** series of Bible studies:

Preparing My Heart for Advent

Preparing My Heart for Easter

Preparing My Heart for Motherhood

For more information about this series, visit AMG Publishers on the Web at:

www.amgpublishers.com

PREPARING MY HEART FOR MOTHERHOOD

AMG Publishers

ANN MARIE STEWART

Preparing My Heart for Motherhood:
For Mothers at Any Stage of the Journey

First Printing, 2008

ISBN 13: 978-0-89957-027-3
ISBN 10: 0-89957-027-5

Cover design by Daryle Beam at Bright Boy Design, Chattanooga, TN

Interior design and typesetting by PerfecType, Nashville, TN

Editing and proofreading by Rick Steele

Printed in Canada

13 12 11 10 09 08 –T– 6 5 4 3 2 1

Dedicated to my husband Will
The Daddy of our girls

Acknowledgments

Barbara Curtis, Jill Dye, Kay Vanderwerf, Jane Eskew, Sherrill Kraakmo, Veronica Hall, Leslie Sogandares, Joan McClenny, Jen Gilfillan, Sandra, Lydia Harris, Carrie Leslie, Christy Slone, Debbie Winkle, Tina Fetterly, Jodie Musgrove, Karen Marrs, Becky Viera, Kristen Smith, Maria Reinertson, Xandra Esko, Aimee Morgan, Anne Miller, Rachelle Knight, Marci Andrews, Kim Domin, Katie Ensloe, Polly Nagell, Maureen Erickson, Holly Coe, Barb Boughton, Lori Galloway, Caroline Roetcisoender, Kristy Schnabel, Brandy Conomea, Lisa Pinkham, Elizabeth DeBarros, Karen McAndrews, Dr. Edyth Phillips, Anita Faull, Laura Edelbrock, Joanne Sampl, Glenn and Helen Garner, Leslie Williams, Debbie Marshall, Karen van der Riet, Bill and Ruth Roetcisoender, Milt Harris, Nancy Fisler, Veronica Hall, Jennifer Sorensen, Janet Wilkie, Char Jacobson, Joan Lundquist, Melissa Hanson, Beverly Heller, Lois Parker, and Mary Kate White. Many thanks and much love to my husband Will and daughters Christine and Julia for the privilege of being a mother. And finally, Lydia Harris, Rick Steele, and Dan Penwell for their editing assistance.

About the Author

ANN MARIE STEWART is the author of *Preparing My Heart for Advent: A Spiritual Pilgrimage for the Christmas Season, Preparing My Heart for Easter: A Woman's Journey to the Cross and Beyond*, and writes a bi-monthly column titled "*Ann's Lovin' Ewe.*"

While completing her Masters in film and television at the University of Michigan, Ann directed award-winning film and video productions. Ann's twelve years of teaching music and English prepare her to present a study that is easy to follow.

Ann and her husband, Will, and two daughters, Christine and Julia, run a small sheep farm in Paeonian Springs, Virginia. While writing this study, their ewes gave birth to over twenty lambs, and Bonnie their sheep dog gave birth to eight puppies. Talk about preparing for motherhood! With anecdotes from mothering, teaching, and farming, Ann is an expressive and engaging speaker and singer for groups of all ages. More information can be found at: www.PreparingMyHeart.com

Introduction

For me to write a book about motherhood might imply I have it all together. I don't.

Neither do any of the friends and family listed in this study. When I began writing this study, I wasn't certain what the table of contents would contain. But as mothers answered, "What do you wish you had known before you became a parent?" the study took shape. In this study you'll "hear" them talk talking about loving God with all your heart, encouraging you to love your husband, discussing changes motherhood brings, and describing how your heart can be filled to overflowing so you love your children. You'll learn from their stories and experiences and also read the Word so you can treasure truths in your heart.

Jesus' mother Mary also treasured things in her heart. Luke writes that after the shepherds visited her, *"Mary kept all these things, and pondered them in her heart"* (Luke 2:19). And again, years later, after a youthful Jesus was discovered teaching in the temple, Luke writes, *"But his mother kept all these sayings in her heart"* (Luke 2:51).

What does it mean to treasure? To ponder? To keep something in your heart? Treasuring truths may prepare or refresh you in your journey of motherhood. Each day you'll have a little *homework*—called *Heartwork*. This study includes ample room to take notes and record personal insights and treasures.

Sit down with a cup of tea or coffee and get ready for a complex and wonderful journey. Ask God to teach you to number your days that you may gain a heart of wisdom (Psalms 90:12). And like Mary, may your hearts treasure and ponder all God wants to teach you.

Suggestions for Leaders

To gather a group of women for your study, why not consider having a Motherhood Shower or Refresher Course for Moms? Perhaps over the next few weeks, you can host your own Mother's Day shower and see what truths your friends and family share with each other. Nobody has to be expecting a child, but their *presence* could also include *presents* for the local women's shelter or pregnancy clinic.

In the invitation, include the following questions.

1. If you were five steps ahead and could advise someone walking behind you, what would you tell them about how to pack for the journey of motherhood?
2. What can a mother-to-be think about now that might prepare her heart?
3. What has God taught you in this role that might help someone who is going to be a mother or who is already a mother?
4. What scripture or passage has come to life in new ways since becoming a mother? Do you have a family life verse or motto?
5. Who is your role model as a wife/Mom? Why?
6. How would you like to be remembered as a wife and Mom?

Each guest can bring scrapbooks to jog her memory. Celebrate motherhood through food, fellowship, and sharing. Close your shower with a prayer from Psalm 139:13–16:

> *For you created my inmost being; you knit me together in my mother's womb. I praise you because I am fearfully and wonderfully made; your works are wonderful, I know that full well. My frame was not hidden from you when I was made in the secret place. When I was woven together in the depths of the earth, your eyes saw my unformed body. All the days ordained for me were written in your book before one of them came to be.*

As your motherhood group continues to meet, focus on how to put into practice the truths learned from the lessons. May this study bless you as a leader and may your group be encouraged in their journey of motherhood.

Contents

A Heart for God

Do you realize God knew you before the creation of the world? He loves you and has a plan for your life? When our children know they are loved, they feel more secure and confident. The benefits of feeling loved are just as true for you. Knowing you are loved and someone believes in you gives hope and inspiration.

This week we begin by focusing on having a heart for God by recognizing how He loves us. This security causes us to look to Him and be still in His presence as we spend time talking to Him. We will hear the stories of Barbara, Jill, Veronica, Joan, and Lydia, and learn what God taught them about motherhood. As you read their stories, think about how to apply the godly principles they've learned in your own relationship with God and with your children.

A Heart for God . . .

Is Loved by God—Barbara
Is Chosen by God—Jill
Looks to God—Veronica
Is Still before God—Joan
Talks to God—Lydia

Your first child changes your name to Mommy and teaches you innumerable lessons. But what if you multiplied those lessons by twelve?

My friend Barbara is mother of a dozen children. Wouldn't you love to hear Barbara answer the question, "What do you wish you had known before you became a mom?" Would she answer with twelve times the wisdom?

"For I know the plans I have for you," declares the LORD, "plans to prosper you and not to harm you, plans to give you hope and a future. Then you will call upon me

and come and pray to me, and I will listen to you. You will seek me and find me when you seek me with all your heart." (Jeremiah 29:11–13)

Day One — A Heart for God... Is Loved by God—Barbara

Barbara lacked an earthly father and mother who could model good parenting. When Barbara was five, her father left the family, and her mother filled the gap with booze and men. At the age of eight, after Barbara was placed in foster care, Barbara was sexually abused. Later, when returned to a mother who could barely provide for her children's physical and emotional needs, eleven-year-old Barbara was in charge of her family's groceries, cleaning, and laundry. Still, Barbara dreamed and imagined. Too poor to decorate her bedroom, she cut out the pastel portraits of little girls on the Northern® bathroom tissue, taped them to her wall, and hoped that one day she would have twelve children of her own.

After Barbara married and expected her first child, she longed to share her love with that baby, but was devastated when she miscarried. She later gave birth to two daughters, and wanting to rise above her past, pursued an education, eventually becoming a Montessori teacher. But in the 1970s she became involved in radical politics and drugs. Her marriage ended in divorce, and an abortion followed. Barbara became the serial addict, alcoholic, and neglectful, promiscuous mother she swore she would never be.

Though doctors had told her she would be unable to conceive again, she became pregnant and married the baby's father. Tripp and Barbara later became Christians, and their family grew—and grew. When her eighth child was placed in Barbara's arms, the beautiful almond eyes gazing back at her were simply awe-inspiring. At that moment, she decided that because God entrusted her with a son with Down syndrome, "God must love me so much!" One year later, Barbara gave birth to Madeleine. Barb and Tripp then adopted three boys with Down syndrome.

Barbara no longer decorates with pictures of children she doesn't know. Instead she has twelve framed school pictures of her own children, spanning three decades, lining the top of her piano.

In addition to her career spent wearing the apron in the house, Barbara is a well-known blogger and the author of nine books and over seven hundred articles. Though her voice is sweet and youthful, her words are strong—at times prophetic, at times filled with hope, and always authentic.

Though Barbara lacked a loving earthly father and mother, she did have a heavenly Father. And so to the question, "What do you wish you had known before you became a mom?" Barbara answers, "I wish I had known God loved me and had a plan for my life."

Heartwork

What about you? Can you grasp the depth of His love for you? Do you know that He has a purpose for your life? Let's read on and learn more about God's fatherly and motherly characteristics.

1. Zephaniah 3:17 states, "The LORD your God is with you, he is mighty to save. He will take great delight in you, he will quiet you with his love, he will rejoice over you with singing." According to this verse, what are five ways your heavenly Father wants to show His love?

_____

_____

_____

_____

_____

2. In this passage from Hosea 11:1–4, God describes His relationship with Israel. Underline the words and phrases that show His actions are like a Father's.

> *When Israel was a child, I loved him, and out of Egypt I called my son. But the more I called Israel, the further they went from me. They sacrificed to the Baals and they burned incense to images. It was I who taught Ephraim to walk, taking them by the arms; but they did not realize it was I who healed them. I led them with cords of human kindness, with ties of love; I lifted the yoke from their neck and bent down to feed them.*

God's actions show He is a protective Father with motherly tenderness. My friend Brandy wrote that when she had a three-year-old and twin one-year-olds, she studied Psalm 91 and found it so comforting.

It makes you feel special and loved to be a child of God. Motherhood gives us a glimpse of His paternal love as we feel such love for our own children. I love to read it, and I recently shared it with my now seven-year-old twin daughter. After I read it, she said, 'That just makes you feel good when you read it, doesn't it?' Exactly. —*Brandy*

📖 3. Like Brandy's daughter, read the following portion from Psalm 91 and "feel good." What things will God do, according to these verses?

_____

_____

_____

He who dwells in the shelter of the Most High will rest in the shadow of the Almighty. I will say of the LORD, "He is my refuge and my fortress, my God, in whom I trust." Surely he will save you from the fowler's snare and from the deadly pestilence. He will cover you with his feathers, and under his wings you will find refuge; his faithfulness will be your shield and rampart.

> "The eternal God is your refuge, and underneath are the everlasting arms."
> (Deuteronomy 33:27a)

God's love is expressed in both paternal and maternal ways. Isaiah 66:13 says, "As a mother comforts her child, so will I comfort you." One of the most intimate moments is when a mother holds a baby at her breast. Isaiah 49 takes this scene and explains that God's love goes beyond even this tender scene.

But Zion said, "The LORD has forsaken me, the Lord has forgotten me." "Can a mother forget the baby at her breast and have no compassion on the child she has borne? Though she may forget, I will not forget you! See, I have engraved you on the palms of my hands; your walls are ever before me." (Isaiah 49:14–16)

How do you know God cannot forget your name? You are engraved on the palms of His hands.

4. Who on earth loves you most?

_____

Can you imagine God's love is even greater?

_____

_____

5. Underline the words "I will not forget you!" from Isaiah 49, above, and don't forget them!

> "Greater love has no one than this, that he lay down his life for his friends."
> (John 15:13)

Not only is God's protective paternal and comforting maternal love described; Jesus demonstrated His tender love when He entered Jerusalem. He knew His followers couldn't understand that He brought peace. He knew He would be crucified. Nevertheless, He compared Himself to a mother.

> *O Jerusalem, Jerusalem, you who kill the prophets and stone those sent to you, how often I have longed to gather your children together, as a hen gathers her chicks under her wings, but you were not willing. (Matthew 27:37)*

6. In the above portion, underline the words that show Jesus' loving, motherly actions and characteristics.

7. What additional words from the Old Testament prophet Isaiah show the tenderness of Jesus, our Good Shepherd? Underline them.

> *He tends his flock like a shepherd: He gathers the lambs in his arms and carries them close to his heart; he gently leads those that have young. (Isaiah 40:11)*

God is your Father and longs to carry you close to His heart. You are a child of God. "How great is the love the Father has lavished on us, that we should be called children of God! And that is what we are!" (1 John 3:1). No matter what your upbringing, you have a heavenly Father who loves you, and desires to give you good and perfect gifts (James 1:17), so you can rest in His care. Jesus even said, "If you then, though you are evil, know how to give good gifts to your children, how much more will your Father in heaven give good gifts to those who ask him!" (Matthew 7:11). And if you understand that He has a plan for your life, like Barbara, you can look for the good He is doing, no matter what your circumstances.

8. Journal your thoughts below. How does it help to know God can take your past and give you purpose? How could knowing He is a good and caring Father with motherly tenderness change your parenting? How does it make you feel to know He loves you more than you love your own child?

_____

_____

_____

I've turned two of Paul's writings into a prayer. Try praying His word for you and your child. (Romans 8:38–39; Ephesians 3:17–19)

Response: *Lord, help me grasp the width and depth and height and length of Your love for me and show me how to share Your love with my children. Help me know Your love that surpasses knowledge—that I may be filled to the measure of all the fullness of God and spill forth with His love. For I am convinced that neither death nor life, neither angels nor demons, neither the present nor the future, nor any powers, neither height nor depth, nor anything else in all creation, will be able to separate me from Your love. Thank you for that love. Help me to teach my children that they will never be separated from Your love. In Jesus' Name, Amen*

R♒

After my husband Will and I married, we settled into a newly formed, small church group. Although most of the members later moved away, we remain close friends. Why? Because we supported and comforted each other through so many of life's challenges: the deaths of parents, moves, infertility, as well as the joy of new babies. My friend Jill and her husband Jeff were also members of that small group with a big heart. Through this group we were again reminded of God's plans—that we were chosen and loved with an everlasting love.

A Heart for God… Is Chosen by God—Jill

> *In him we were also chosen, having been predestined according to the plan of him who works out everything in conformity with the purpose of his will, in order that we, who were the first to hope in Christ, might be **for the praise of his glory.** And you also were included in Christ when you heard the word of truth, the gospel of your salvation. Having believed, you were marked in him with a seal, the promised Holy Spirit, who is a deposit guaranteeing our inheritance until the redemption of those who are God's possession—**to the praise of his glory.** (Ephesians 1:11–14; emphasis added)*

Jill longed for a child. Day after day she cried out to God, "Have you forgotten me?" On the day Jeff and Jill were to find out the results of their in-vitro fertilization, our small church group scheduled a "Celebrating God's Will" party and served up the couple's favorite foods from Outback Steakhouse®. Would this medical intervention end thirteen years of waiting?

> "Religion that God our Father accepts as pure and faultless is this: to look after orphans and widows in their distress and to keep oneself from being polluted by the world."
>
> (James 1:27)

Though the test came back negative and they were not pregnant, we celebrated God's will, not yet knowing that God had a different and even bigger plan. On the way home from the party, Jeff said they needed to look into adoption. But for Jill, the "what ifs" weighed heavily.

Nevertheless, they completed the paperwork for a domestic adoption, and then the agency pressed them to go international. Their friends thought "quiet and reserved" Jeff and Jill would match up perfectly with a sweet little girl from China. But as Jill looked at her freshly painted nursery with the blue Peter Rabbit border, the picture of an angel standing over a sleeping boy, and a blue-framed picture with the words "God danced the day you were born," she whispered, "This looks like a *boy's* room!"

In fact, a pregnant couple from their own state had chosen Jeff and Jill to parent their unborn child. On January 6, 1999, their son was born, and on February 3, James came home to his little boy's room.

Somehow in the suddenness, Jill realized she had missed nine months of pregnancy and bonding. It almost seemed she had kidnapped baby James and she was caring for someone *else's* baby. "Then God impressed upon me that I was! James was not my own, He was God's, and I was to take care of him!" That wasn't all God would teach her. Five months later, on July 7, as Jill adjusted to bottles and diapers, the adoption agency called with the news, "Your little Chinese girl is now available!"

"But we put the papers on hold!" Jill exclaimed, cradling six-month-old James in her arms. Not only had the adoption agency neglected to put their papers on hold, the agency policy didn't even allow two adoptions in the same year! Now that Jeff and Jill were down to a single income, the thought of two babies sounded overwhelming. And with no family in the area to care for James, how could they travel to China? Too many more *what-ifs*.

"Could I at least see the picture of the baby girl I would have gotten?" Jill asked tentatively. That evening Jill watched as Jeff repeatedly returned to the kitchen to sneak peeks at the baby's photo. Who could turn down the little girl dressed in pink, smiling so sweetly back at them with a look that said, "Bring me home!" Her left hand was blurry as if she were waving her first hello to her new parents. They had two days to decide.

Because the baby was eighteen months old, and outside the age window Jeff and Jill had requested, the Chinese government would not take offense if they rejected the adoption. But was it merely a "clerical error?" And was it also a "coincidence" that her birth date was January 6, exactly one year before their James' January 6 birth date?

Two days later, when Jill called Jeff at work, he exclaimed, "We're going to China!" And so, quiet Jeff and Jill, for whom a trip from Virginia to nearby Pennsylvania was a big excursion, put their baby in the arms of friends from their small group and flew to China in the middle of an August typhoon. The airplane in front of them crash-landed, and torrential flooding thwarted Jeff and Jill's efforts to reach their daughter that day.

But on August 23, Jeff, Jill, and James welcomed "Little Jade" (another "J" name) into their family and added the biblical first name *Lydia*. As they looked back on the year, they realized that Lydia was born forty weeks after they'd celebrated God's will and decided to adopt. Their Chinese daughter was conceived at the same time they were told their in-vitro had failed. Adoption required Jill to let God be in control and to trust in Him with all her heart. After all, her children are truly His children and His plans are bigger and better than all of Jill's *what-ifs*.

Heartwork

Today you'll take a look at three biblical adoptions: Moses, Jesus, and you!

As the Israelite population multiplied, Pharaoh feared the Israelite's strength and thus enslaved and oppressed them. Later, he even ordered the midwives to kill all the baby boys born to the Hebrews. When the midwives failed to obey, Pharaoh gave an order that every boy born must be thrown into the Nile (Exodus 1). Then Moses was born.

Exodus 2:1–10

Now a man of the house of Levi married a Levite woman, and she became pregnant and gave birth to a son. When she saw that he was a fine child, she hid him for three months. But when she could hide him no longer, she got a papyrus basket for him and coated it with tar and pitch. Then she placed the child in it and put it among the reeds along the bank of the Nile. His sister stood at a distance to see what would happen to him.

Then Pharaoh's daughter went down to the Nile to bathe, and her attendants were walking along the river bank. She saw the basket among the reeds and sent her slave girl to get it. She opened it and saw the baby. He was crying, and she felt sorry for him. "This is one of the Hebrew babies," she said.

Then his sister asked Pharaoh's daughter, "Shall I go and get one of the Hebrew women to nurse the baby for you?"

"Yes, go," she answered. And the girl went and got the baby's mother.

Pharaoh's daughter said to her, "Take this baby and nurse him for me, and I will pay you." So the woman took the baby and nursed him. When the child grew older, she took him to Pharaoh's daughter and he became her son. She named him Moses, saying, "I drew him out of the water."

1. What would it take for Moses' mother to place him in a basket in the Nile River? What did her actions ensure?

_____

_____

2. Moses entered the very home of the Pharaoh who condemned baby boys to death. What is ironic about the identity of the nursemaid? (verse 8).

_____

_____

_____

The story does not end with this first miraculous rescue. God placed Moses in that location at that time so He could free the Israelites and take them out of Egypt in yet another miraculous rescue complete with plagues and the parting of the Red Sea. Moses led the Israelites in the desert for forty years and eventually their descendants entered the Promised Land. God had a purpose and a plan for Moses' adoption.

Consider the implications. Moses was saved because his mother relinquished him. Moses was pulled from the reeds and adopted by Pharaoh's daughter. Her actions, too, saved his life. Moses had contact with both his biological mom as well as his adoptive mom, something we now call "open adoption."

Moses is also a forerunner of Jesus. God gave up His son

for a purpose. Joseph became Jesus' adoptive father on earth and consistently obeyed God's plan for him to parent and protect Mary's son. Throughout the ages, Jesus has led followers to the promised land of heaven.

3. How would it feel to be the adoptive father of the Son of God?

_____

_____

_____

4. What character qualities was God looking for in Jesus' earthly father?

_____

_____

_____

_____

God chose a man who listened and obeyed. Because Joseph followed God's directions, Joseph, Mary, and baby Jesus were repeatedly protected. With Joseph playing such a key role in the life of baby Jesus, we see a beautiful example of God's perspective on adoption and the blessing of "chosenness."

Because Jill wanted James and Lydia to know how special they are to her and to God and to understand their "chosenness," Jill created two beautiful photo albums that told their adoption stories. Jill reads each book over and over to them so they understand how deeply they are loved.

> As God has put us under his Covenant, we (the adoptive family) are under a covenant, a binding agreement, also with our children to protect, love, and care for them unconditionally. —Jill

We all have a similar book. The Bible explains how we've been chosen and loved. It explains that the names of believers are written in His book of life (Revelation 3:5; 13:8; 20:12) and that we are adopted into God's family when we believe in His Son.

> Yet to all who received him, to those who believed in his name, he gave the right to become children of God—children born not of natural descent, nor of human decision or a husband's will, but born of God (John 1:12–13).

Though Jill and Jeff *knew* they had been adopted into God's family, they couldn't *comprehend* it until God was the author of their adoptions. Perhaps you have not adopted a child, but if you have received Him and believe in His name, you are "not born of natural descent" but "born of God." You're adopted and can call out "Daddy, Daddy!" or "Abba, Father!"

> *But when the time had fully come, God sent his Son, born of a woman, born under law, to redeem those under law, that we might receive the full rights of sons. Because you are sons, God sent the Spirit of his Son into our hearts, the Spirit who calls out, "Abba, Father." So you are no longer a slave, but a son; and since you are a son, God has made you also an heir. (Galatians 4:4–7)*

5. Romans 8:14–18 also confirms we can call Him *Daddy*. Underline every phrase that shows as a believer you are a son of God, or an heir.

> *Because those who are led by the Spirit of God are sons of God. For you did not receive a spirit that makes you a slave again to fear, but you received the Spirit of sonship. And by him we cry, "Abba, Father." The Spirit himself testifies with our spirit that we are God's children. Now if we are children, then we are heirs—heirs of God and co-heirs with Christ, if indeed we share in his sufferings in order that we may also share in his glory.*
>
> *I consider that our present sufferings are not worth comparing with the glory that will be revealed in us.*

6. Besides being called "children of God," (1 John 3:2; 5:2), we have other names. Read 1 Peter 2:9–10 below and underline all the words that say *who* we are.

> *But you are a chosen people, a royal priesthood, a holy nation, a people belonging to God, **that you may declare the praises of him** who called you out of darkness into*

> *I heard once adoption is a scriptural metaphor that emphasizes our rights as God's children. Being 'adopted' to Jeff and me means Lydia and James are permanently in our family, just as we are in God's. I like the word permanent! —Jill*

his wonderful light. Once you were not a people, but now you are the people of God; once you had not received mercy, but now you have received mercy. (emphasis added)

7. Because we are chosen and adopted, we have a purpose. According to the previous verses, what is it?

_____

_____

_____

_____

8. The following passage confirms we are instruments of praise. Underline the words from Ephesians 1:4–6 which bring you comfort.

> *For he chose us in him before the creation of the world to be holy and blameless in his sight. In love he predestined us to be adopted as his sons through Jesus Christ, in accordance with his pleasure and will—to the **praise of his glorious grace**, which he has freely given us in the One he loves. (emphasis added)*

Perhaps one of the most freeing prayers you can pray is to tell God *your* children are *His*. And perhaps one of the most inspiring thoughts is that *you* are chosen! Bring purpose to your life by bringing Him the glory and declaring the praises of Jesus.

9. Journal below how these thoughts will affect your parenting.

_____

_____

_____

10. What book of love can you create for your children to reinforce concepts you've learned from yesterday and today?

_____

_____

_____

Response: *Lord, help me to remember that all of my "what-ifs" have answers in You. May I trust You more each day and listen* *to Your directions. As I follow Your leadership, protect my family and guide us all in the way we should go. Help me see that You have a plan for my life and the lives of my children. As your adopted child I know I can trust You and Your care for me. Today may I find my purpose in You and praise You for all that You have done in Christ Jesus. May my praise bring glory to Your name. Thank You for adopting me!*

Knowing we are loved and chosen, gives us the security to look to Him for our strength. Because my friend Veronica lives in the *other* Washington, and a continent separates us, we're united mainly by e-mail. Her Bible study groups have test-driven my published Easter study (*Preparing My Heart for Easter* [2006, AMG Publishers]) as well as the one you're reading right now. Veronica is a mother of four whose heart looks to God.

> *"This is what the LORD says, he who made the earth, the LORD who formed it and established it—the LORD is his name: 'Call to me and I will answer you and tell you great and unsearchable things you do not know.'"* (Jeremiah 33:2–3)

Day Three	**A Heart for God...** Looks to God—Veronica

When I asked Veronica what to pack for parenting, she answered, "Pack light. Anything you pack will be inadequate; plan on needing God. Nothing can prepare you fully. Motherhood is truly walking moment by moment hanging onto the Father. Only He can guide you through." Veronica discovered that truth almost immediately after the birth of her first child.

Baby Elizabeth's delivery necessitated an emergency C-section. The day Veronica's husband David brought her and Elizabeth home, Veronica was not allowed to get off the couch or lift anything heavier than her seven-pound, four-ounce daughter. But they hadn't arranged for anyone to stay with her and the baby. Like most women, Veronica had always thought her mom would be there to help her, but her mother died right before Veronica found out she was pregnant.

Now Veronica was home with the baby and David had to leave for work. Unfortunately, because both Veronica and David had just been laid off within the last year, this was a very difficult time financially. Dave had just started a new full commission job and wasn't making much of anything yet.

> "Do you not know? Have you not heard? The LORD is the everlasting God, the Creator of the ends of the earth. He will not grow tired or weary, and his understanding no one can fathom. He gives strength to the weary and increases the power of the weak."
> (Isaiah 40:28–29)

> I so clearly remember David looking at me, not knowing what to do, and hoping I would fix the problem, "Well, can't you call someone?" My mother had died of cancer, my sister was unavailable, and I couldn't think of what I could do. I was in complete fear and panic. How was I going to care for this infant? What crazy person allowed me to bring this fragile, adorable child home? I was not prepared!
> —Veronica

But God ran to Veronica's side. "For I am the LORD, your God, who takes hold of your right hand and says to you, Do not fear; I will help you" (Isaiah 41:13).

Veronica eventually called her sister-in-law Janice, who was taking care of Veronica's dad.

> My dad answered the phone. When I asked for Janice, I began to cry. He said she was out and asked what was wrong. I told him my predicament, and he asked if I would like him to come. It hadn't even crossed my mind! "Oh, dad, could you?! Would you know what to do?" He assured me he had cared for all of us, was well experienced, and would be right over.
>
> My memories of him caring for us that afternoon until Dave could return are some of my sweetest memories. And then one month later, he lay dying of heart failure—a sudden

> "He tends his flock like a shepherd: He gathers the lambs in his arms and carries them close to his heart; he gently leads those that have young."
> (Isaiah 40:11)

occurrence from a simple medical procedure—and Elizabeth and I said our last goodbyes to him. We were the only ones available as my sister and brother were both out of town. Again, I felt so alone, but knew my God was with me and would help me raise my family and face whatever else the future held. —*Veronica*

As Veronica's children continue to grow through stages, God has run to Veronica's side many more times.

> *In our information-driven culture, it's difficult to recognize that no matter how much our well-meaning friends or we know about a particular child-rearing issue, God always knows infinitely more. He loves our children more perfectly than we ever can. He knows what our kids need and can help us meet those needs if we trust in Him and seek His wisdom*—**Barb**

Every child is unique in personality and needs; it makes me wish children came with a manual. There are children who know how to push your buttons, teenagers who can rattle your world, that child who is so like you that it frightens you. There are the times you find yourself crying on your pillow, because you see how far you fell short just that day, and then God's Word flows back that He shores up the broken places, reminding me that I don't have to be the perfect mom—just the mom trusting him and walking where He leads. —*Veronica*

Like Veronica, you need to trust God and entrust your child to Him. That starts with developing a relationship with God. How can you help your child know God if you don't know Him?

Carrie, whose story you will read in the week: "A Changed Heart" wrote that when *you* look to God, so will your *child*.

I realized that a child's relationship with a parent gives them an initial view of what God is like. Granted more often the father has the greater burden here, but mothers, too, show Jesus to our kids. Our relationship with the Lord has such an influence. This has been heavy on my heart at times, as each of us are flawed, but it also showed me in all things how God wants us to depend on Him in everything. Even as a mother, my first priority is my relationship with Him. He strengthens and nurtures me, and I in turn can nurture my child. I build a relationship with Him and my child can see how to relate to Him. —*Carrie*

As God strengthens and nurtures you, you can in turn nurture your child. What does your relationship with God look like to your child? You are writing a letter on his heart.

> *You yourselves are our letter, written on our hearts, known and read by everybody. You show that you are a letter from Christ, the result of our ministry, written not with ink but with the Spirit of the living God, not on tablets of stone but on tablets of human hearts. (2 Corinthians 3:2–3)*

1. What letter will you write (or are you currently writing) on your child's heart?

_____

_____

_____

_____

Being able to rely on God comes from knowing Him well enough to know He'll come through. Do you know Him that well? When my seven-year-old nephew Tim filled out an elementary questionnaire, *What does your mom do well?*, he answered, "God."

His surprised mom was tickled he felt that way about her. After all, it was much more complimentary than his answer about what she smelled like (a tin can!).

2. How might your children boast about you?

_____

_____

_____

_____

The following verses from Jeremiah remind you to place a priority on your relationship with God. All the other things you might boast about fall short of knowing Him.

> *This is what the lord says:*
> *"Let not the wise man boast of his wisdom or the strong man boast of his strength or the rich man boast*

of his riches, but let him who boasts boast about this: that he understands and knows me, that I am the lord, who exercises kindness, justice and righteousness on earth, for in these I delight," declares the Lord. (Jeremiah 9:23–24)

Knowing the Lord is one of the best gifts you give yourself and your child. My neighbor Katie, with her toddler son and baby daughter, loves being a mom. It's fun to watch her in the beginning of her journey. And yet, what she has discovered mirrors what Veronica and so many others have said about reading God's Word.

> It has become so apparent to me how vital it is I am in the Word and model for my child what it means to walk with the Lord—or at least do my best. I have also been reminded how the Lord blesses us—his children—for studying His word. What a gift to pass along to our children. So this piece of scripture has spoken to me recently. "I have no greater joy than to hear that my children are walking in the truth" (3 John 1:4). *—Katie*

3. Do you have a favorite Bible verse? How does it encourage you?

_____

_____

_____

As a mom, you may feel overwhelmed by situations and become fearful. Instead, you need to claim verses that offer consolation and strength. Some of Veronica's favorites are below. Underline encouraging phrases. Circle one or two verses and commit them to memory.

> *He alone is my rock and my salvation; he is my fortress, I will never be shaken. (Psalms 62:2)*

> *So do not fear, for I am with you; do not be dismayed, for I am your God. I will strengthen you and help you; I will uphold you with my righteous right hand. (Isaiah 41:10)*

> *Since you are my rock and my fortress, for the sake of your name lead and guide me. (Psalms 31:3)*

The LORD is my rock, my fortress and my deliverer; my God is my rock, in whom I take refuge. He is my shield and the horn of my salvation, my stronghold. (Psalms 18:2)

He who fears the LORD has a secure fortress, and for his children it will be a refuge. (Proverbs 14:26)

I have set the LORD always before me. Because he is at my right hand, I will not be shaken. Therefore my heart is glad and my tongue rejoices; my body also will rest secure. (Psalms 16:8–9)

The LORD is my light and my salvation— whom shall I fear? The LORD is the stronghold of my life—of whom shall I be afraid? (Psalms 27:1)

God is our refuge and strength, an ever-present help in trouble. Therefore we will not fear, though the earth give way and the mountains fall into the heart of the sea, though its waters roar and foam and the mountains quake with their surging. (Psalms 46:1–3)

> *Take time to revitalize yourself in His word. My Bible studies force me to make that time. Otherwise, I would probably lack the discipline to carve out time with all the other tasks that come with making a home and nurturing your family.* —*Katie*

Carve out time with Him so you can nurture your family. Look to Him for rest and renewal. Then you will not grow weary but will soar on wings like an eagle!

"Come to me, all you who are weary and burdened, and I will give you rest. Take my yoke upon you and learn from me, for I am gentle and humble in heart, and you will find rest for your souls. For my yoke is easy and my burden is light." (Matthew 11:28–30)

Even youths grow tired and weary, and young men stumble and fall; but those who hope in the LORD will renew their strength. They will soar on wings like eagles; they will run and not grow weary, they will walk and not be faint. (Isaiah 40:30–31)

Today's prayer is based on these two passages.

Response: *Lord, sometimes I feel weary and burdened. You are gentle and humble in heart, so help me find rest for my soul. Your yoke is easy and Your burden is light. May I take on Your yoke and learn from you. As I put my hope in You, renew my strength. Help me soar on wings like eagles and run without growing weary, and walk without fainting.*

While nine months pregnant with my first child, I conducted December concerts with a new awareness of being "great with child." I claimed, "It ain't over until the fat lady sings." At 2:00 AM on December 20, after four concerts and a church event, my water broke, the power went out in our townhouse, and Christine Alane was born, ending my fast-paced career as a high-school music teacher.

That Christmas, as a new mother, I savored a quiet, slow pace and watched my daughter Christine sleep in her Stewart plaid-decorated cradle. Though the learning curve was steep and motherhood had challenges, for the first time in my life, I realized I suddenly had no preference for weekdays or weekends. All days were weekends!

Of course, now as my girls grow up, they are involved in everything, and the pace of our life feels hurried and scurried. And for those of you parenting teenagers all going in different directions, you might feel you're living four or five lives in one. And the term "hurry sickness" might feel relevant to you. How do you make your home a haven in the midst of the hurry? That is the focus in my cousin Joan's home. As you look to God for your strength, spend time being still in His presence.

"Be still, and know that I am God; I will be exalted among the nations, I will be exalted in the earth." The Lord *Almighty is with us; the God of Jacob is our fortress.* (Psalm 46:10–11)

Most of Joan's childhood was a training ground for parenting. For seven years, Joan watched her mother die of cancer. In eighth grade, when Joan lost her mother, she became housekeeper and cook altogether too soon. When she left home for college, she immediately plunged into a skydiving adventure, and I had to wonder if it wasn't a direct flight from too much responsibility too early.

After beginning her career as a teacher, Joan married Ed, and they had four beautiful children. Ed had a powerful job that took him all over the world and made family time a challenge. They wanted their home to be a haven and have more time to "*Be still and know that I am God.*" This prompted Ed to launch his own company. Though this allowed him to set his own hours, it meant a new financial investment and strain, and he had to secure his own health insurance—with only catastrophic coverage.

During this time, Joan was diagnosed with breast cancer. The doctor said if her cancer had gone undetected one more month, it would have been terminal. This was indeed catastrophic. Though the news was devastating, the family tried to see God's hand in the picture. Ed sat the kids down and explained that God works all things together for good. They would all need to see how God's hand was working in the situation and keep their eyes open for the good God was doing. They had to be still and watch. As Joan went through a mastectomy, chemotherapy, hysterectomy, radiation, and hormone therapy, the pace of the family slowed.

"He makes me lie down in green pastures, he leads me beside quiet waters, he restores my soul." (Psalm 23:2–3)

One advantage of having cancer was that I had to clear everything off my schedule while I was going through treatment. When treatment was over, I realized how nice it was living at a slower pace with fewer commitments. I became very careful and prayerful about choosing what activities to add to my schedule. I find I need to zealously guard against getting over-busy. —*Joan*

I understand my cousin's feelings. There are many days that feel "over-busy." I feel like a drill sergeant. "Time to get up—hurry, there's fifteen minutes before the bus comes—put your lunch in your backpack—quick—hurry and eat your breakfast—you have two minutes to brush your teeth!" Then as soon as they get off the bus, "Practice your piano—how much homework do you have?—we have to be at softball in fifteen minutes—get that done before Dad comes home—hurry and play FAST so you can go to bed on time."

And so I think every family appreciates a slower pace and fewer commitments. Moms and kids rejoice over a December snow day or an evening when the power goes out, even if it cancels a fun event. Sometimes you just have to reserve time for what is important. A month before Christmas, Joan's family sits down and crosses off days on the calendar. These are reserved for family evenings.

Joan explains,

> We do make an effort to not let life get too hectic. When the kids were younger, we focused on sports and activities the whole family could enjoy together, and we tried to avoid having everyone running off to sport practices or activities that kept us overly busy and separated. We found family skiing was a lot of fun and the AWANA Bible clubs at our church were great because all four kids were at the same place at the same time having fun and learning Bible verses. Swimming, camping, and one-day outings were also big hits. Inviting other families over for dinner and games was another great way to have fun as a family.

Not only do they make their family time a priority, they also have a special time to "be still" each evening.

> Another thing we do as a family that keeps us close and connected is spending some time each evening before bedtime reading from the Bible and praying together. We like to read a short passage, let one child per night ask some questions about the passage (they like to try to stump each other), and then let the questioner choose a topic or concern need to pray about. We keep it short and sweet—about 20 minutes per night. —*Joan*

Heartwork

It doesn't need to take an illness to make your family slow down and recognize what is important. God created a day of rest for a purpose. He wants us to "Be still."

1. Write one of the following verses (emphasis added on all three verses) on a note card and place it someplace where it can remind you to slow down.

> "*The* LORD *will fight for you; you need only to* **be still**." *(Exodus 14:14)*

> "**Be still** *before the* LORD *and wait patiently for him.*" *(Psalm 37:7a)*

> "**Be still***, and know that I am God; I will be exalted among the nations, I will be exalted in the earth.*" *(Psalm 46:10)*

2. List your priorities below. Does the pace of your day correspond to your priorities?

_____

_____

_____

3. What can you do to keep the pace slower and in sync with your priorities?

Psalm 90:12 says, "Teach us to number our days aright, that we may gain a heart of wisdom." Wouldn't it be wonderful to have a heart of wisdom and to number your days appropriately? Jesus should be the Lord of your schedule and of your life.

Jesus Himself spent time with His Father and said, "*Come with me by yourselves to a quiet place and get some rest*" (Mark 6:31). After He and his disciples went by boat to a solitary place, the crowds followed. So Jesus taught, performed a miracle, and fed five thousand men, concluding His day with a retreat for time in prayer. He had a busy day but it was never too hurried to leave out time with His Father.

> "There remains, then, a Sabbath-rest for the people of God; for anyone who enters God's rest also rests from his own work, just as God did from his. Let us, therefore, make every effort to enter that rest." (Hebrews 4:9–11)

If Jesus is saying to you, "Come with me by yourselves to a quiet place and get some rest," can you plan a time and place? My friend Barbara Curtis recognizes the challenges of quiet times for new moms in her book, *Lord, Meet Me in the Laundry Room* (2004, Beacon Hill). Susanna Wesley, mother of nineteen, had her quiet time with her apron over her head. Her kids understood that was Mother's time with God, and two of her sons (Charles and John) became the founders of Methodism. Whether an apron, a closet, or the laundry room, plan a special time with Jesus.

4. My date with Jesus:

Time: _____

Place: _____

5. Jesus modeled his values and taught them. Read Luke 10:38–42 below and look for what Jesus considered important.

> *As Jesus and his disciples were on their way, he came to a village where a woman named Martha opened her home to him. She had a sister called Mary, who sat at the Lord's feet listening to what he said. But Martha was distracted by all the preparations that had to be made. She came to him and asked, "Lord, don't you care that my sister has left me to do the work by myself? Tell her to help me!"*
>
> *"Martha, Martha," the Lord answered, "you are worried and upset about many things, but only one thing is needed. Mary has chosen what is better, and it will not be taken away from her."*

6. If Jesus said to you (insert your name) "_____, _____, you are worried and upset about many things, but only one thing is needed." What would that *one thing* be?

_____

_____

7. If you "choose what is better" and "what will not be taken away from you," how could it impact your family?

_____

_____

_____

_____

When your life feels turbulent, remember Jesus is in the boat with you. The disciples were reminded of this during a furious squall on the water when He rebuked the wind and said to the waves, *"Quiet! Be still!"* The wind died down and it was completely calm. (Mark 4:35–41)

8. In what ways do you need to hear Jesus' voice say, *"Quiet! Be still!"* in your life right now?

_____

_____

_____

_____

9. How might your heart preparations bring life to your home? "Above all else, guard your heart, for it is the wellspring of life" (Proverbs 4:23).

_____

_____

_____

Response: *Lord, I'm used to busyness and hurrying from place to place. Help me to re-evaluate my priorities and allow You to order my day so my family is blessed because I spend time in Your presence. Help me not to hurry through the day and miss moments that build relationships with my child. May I be still and know that You are God.*

℞

My friend Polly says if she didn't pray for her three kids each day, it would feel like she was sending them out into the world undressed. Being still in God's presence can involve talking to Him and listening to His voice. If you don't already pray for your children, starting to pray for them even now will yield eternal results.

I will sing of the LORD'S great love forever; with my mouth I will make your faithfulness known through all generations. (Psalm 89:1)

Day Five · A Heart for God... Talks to God—Lydia

Aunt Lydia is a prayer warrior. I can always count on her to pray for me when I send her requests. She recognizes the power of prayer and how it had a profound impact on her life even before she was born.

In 1929 her father, Nicolai Siemens, was imprisoned in Lubjanka prison in Moscow, Russia, and awaited deportation to Siberia. At the same time in Chicago, Illinois, his older brother, Abram, picked up the Chicago *Daily Tribune* and read "Russia Deports 2,000 to Siberia Camps." Certain his brother Nicolai was among them, he called an evening prayer meeting. Sixty prayer warriors kneeled in prayer until Abram said, "We can stop now. I have the conviction God has answered our prayers."

At the very same hour, Nicolai—the man who would become Lydia's father—was miraculously released and reunited with his wife Lena and their newborn son. Days later the three escaped from Russia.

Some time afterward, the family immigrated to the United States (Washington state) with their two sons and then added five daughters. When Lena said she was expecting again, the family was surprised. Her sons predicted, "It's going to be a boy," and then added, "We already have too many girls." But Lena's daughters asked the boys, "Did you pray about it?" The boys hung their heads sheepishly. "We did!" the girls exclaimed, "And we prayed for a girl!" They named this baby sister "Lydia."

The family continued praying for this youngest daughter, and she became a Christian as a preschooler. Lydia went on to marry a godly man and give birth to two children. Lydia realized the importance of praying for her own children from the time they were born, and even more so as little Anita started kindergarten.

Before I took her to school that first day, I felt compelled to pray with her. This began a pattern of praying with Anita, and later also with our son, Jonathan, each morning right before they left for school. Even as teens, they expected my morning prayers. On days when they were running late, they rushed out of their bedrooms and ran down the hall. But they always paused at the top of the landing and said, "Pray, Mom, pray!" I said a quick, "Lord bless and protect them today," gave them a hug, and added, "I love you," as they flew out the door. When I said that first prayer on the first day of kindergarten, I had no idea I was establishing a pattern that would continue until they left home for college. But I'm glad I did. —*Lydia*

> *I* encourage each mom to pray for her children every morning before they leave for preschool, grade school, and throughout high school. Prayer is the best way to protect our children. Start a routine of praying for your children each morning. You won't regret it. —*Lydia*

Lydia's life of prayer prepared her for big changes in her life. In 1988, both of her parents died, and her firstborn left for college. She felt the absence of her parents' prayers but then joined Moms In Touch International, an organization of mothers who pray for their children and their schools. Her prayers extended to a troublesome first-grader her daughter Anita was teaching. One day when Lydia asked how he was doing, to her surprise, Anita said he hadn't been disruptive that day. Instead, he raised his hand and asked questions. When Lydia told her daughter that the Moms in Touch group had prayed for him, Anita answered, "It was obvious." Lydia realized anew that *every* child needs a praying mom.

Later, when Anita faced melanoma and breast cancer in her twenties and early thirties, Lydia found new cause for prayer. And in 2002, Lydia's prayers became even more personal when she herself was diagnosed with incurable but treatable cancer. Then in 2007, when her seventeen-month-old grandson, Owen, faced open-heart surgery, she organized a round-the-clock circle of prayer. God answered her prayers for healing. Anita is doing well, Lydia is in remission, and Owen is an active, happy toddler who loves to pray and says, "Pray Jesus, me." Though we may "pray Jesus me," God

> *I* asked myself, "If I'm not praying for my child, who is?" Unless there's a praying grandmother, aunt, or friend in the child's life, in most cases, the answer is: "No one." —*Lydia*

may not always answer our prayers exactly as we want. But the experience of being still before Him helps us remember that He is in control.

Lydia prays together with her husband daily and encourages her extended family to meet regularly to pray for family needs. "Although my extended family has faced struggles such as illness, alcoholism, and divorce, we've rejoiced in God's blessings of healing, godly marriages, and new births—both physical and spiritual," she says.

Lydia continues,

> *Prayer is the best gift we can give our children. Children outgrow clothes and toys, but they never outgrow their need for our prayers. –Lydia*

Our prayers live on forever, even beyond our lives on earth. Some prayers for our children may be answered when we are no longer here. We can pray ahead, for their careers, marriage partners, and even for future generations. In this way we have an impact upon our descendants yet unborn. I continue to pray that all of my future generations, from now until Jesus returns, will follow God with wholehearted devotion.

We continue to reap the fruit of my parents' faithful prayers. As we follow their example, our prayers become the lasting threads woven into the fabric of future generations.

Heartwork

Lydia's prayer warrior status was strengthened through Moms in Touch International. What a wonderful blessing to pray for your children with other Christian moms. Moms in Touch helps facilitate prayer times by using a format of Praise, Confession, Thanksgiving, and Intercession. www.momsintouch.org. Other groups use a similar format and spell the word A-C-T-S or **A**doration, **C**onfession, **T**hanksgiving, and **S**upplication to help them remember various aspects of prayer.

What does God want to unleash through your prayers? Let's start by reading these verses of adoration aloud (with emphasis added) to our heavenly Father.

Adoration:

Praise the LORD, all his works everywhere in his dominion. *Praise* the LORD, O my soul. *(Psalms 103:22)*

Praise the LORD, O my soul. O LORD my God, you are very great; you are clothed with splendor and majesty. *(Psalms 104:1)*

I will sing to the LORD all my life; I will sing *praise* to my God as long as I live. *(Psalms 104:33)*

Praise the LORD. Give thanks to the LORD, for he is good; his love endures forever. *(Psalms 106:1)*

For great is his love toward us, and the faithfulness of the LORD endures forever. *Praise* the LORD. *(Psalms 117:2)*

May my lips overflow with *praise*, for you teach me your decrees. *(Psalms 119:171)*

Praise the LORD. *Praise* the name of the LORD; *praise* him, you servants of the LORD *(Psalms 135:1)*

Praise the LORD, for the LORD is good; sing *praise* to his name, for that is pleasant. *(Psalms 135:3)*

Great is the LORD and most worthy of *praise*; his greatness no one can fathom. *(Psalms 145:3)*

I will *praise* the LORD all my life; I will sing *praise* to my God as long as I live. *(Psalms 146:2)*

The LORD reigns forever, your God, O Zion, for all generations. *Praise* the LORD. *(Psalms 146:10)*

Praise the LORD. How good it is to sing praises to our God, how pleasant and fitting to *praise* him! *(Psalms 147:1)*

"'As for me, this is my covenant with them," says the LORD. "My Spirit, who is on you, and my words that I have put in your mouth will not depart from your mouth, or from the mouths of your children, or from the mouths of their descendants from this time on and forever,' says the LORD." (Isaiah 59:21)

Add your own praise and adoration by filling in the blanks. Praise God for WHO He is.

God, I praise You because . . .

_____

_____

Jesus I adore you because . . .

_____

_____

Confession:

> If we confess our sins, he is faithful and just and will forgive us our sins and purify us from all unrighteousness. (1 John 1:9)

> Have mercy on me, O God, according to your unfailing love; according to your great compassion blot out my transgressions. Wash away all my iniquity and cleanse me from my sin. (Psalms 51:1–2)

> "He will call upon me, and I will answer him; I will be with him in trouble, I will deliver him and honor him." (Psalms 91:15)

> Cleanse me with hyssop, and I will be clean; wash me, and I will be whiter than snow. (Psalms 51:7)

> Create in me a pure heart, O God, and renew a steadfast spirit within me. (Psalms 51:10)

God, I'm sorry for . . . Please forgive me . . .

Thanksgiving:

> Do not be anxious about anything, but in everything, by prayer and petition, with **thanksgiving**, present your requests to God. (Philippians 4:6)

Lord, Thank you for . . .

Supplication:

Lord, I want to pray for . . .
Lord, help me with . . .

1. In Matthew 6, Jesus offers us a pattern of prayer by prefacing it, "This, then, is how you should pray."

_____

_____

_____

What does each phrase remind you to do in prayer? I've filled in the first answer for you.

"Our Father in heaven, hallowed be your name, (verse 9) *Praise and adore Him*

your kingdom come, your will be done on earth as it is in heaven. (verse 10) _____

Give us today our daily bread. (verse 11)

_____

Forgive us our debts, as we also have forgiven our debtors. (verse 12) _____

And lead us not into temptation, but deliver us from the evil one." (verse 13) _____

In Jesus' prayer, we see that He offers praise to His Father, shows humility, makes a request, models confession, and asks to not be led into temptation.

If you don't know what to pray, remember, the Holy Spirit will help you. Romans 8:26 says, "In the same way, the Spirit helps us in our weakness. We do not know what we ought to pray for, but the Spirit himself intercedes for us with groans that words cannot express."

Jesus gave instructions about *how* and *where* to pray. During Jesus' day, many performed acts of righteousness before men and announced their charity with trumpets. They prayed to be seen. Jesus cautioned against this and said, "When you pray, go into your room, close the door and pray to your Father, who is unseen. Then your Father, who sees what is done in secret, will reward you." (Matthew 6:6).

You can pray anywhere, any time, and in any way. My friend Marci writes, "God is the most relational guy in your life; he likes to be kept up to date about YOU— your thoughts, feelings, opinions. It may feel as if the rest of the world doesn't have time or availability to listen; He does."

> "Ask and it will be given to you; seek and you will find; knock and the door will be opened to you. For everyone who asks receives; he who seeks finds; and to him who knocks, the door will be opened." (Matthew 7:7–8)

> "Be joyful always; pray continually." (1 Thessalonians 5:16–17)

2. Think of a time and place where you can regularly pray. Write it here:

Time: _____

Place: _____

Lydia's father, my grandfather, died at the age of ninety-three after sixty-plus years of marriage to my grandmother Lena. At the funeral home, my Aunt Erna asked my grandmother if she'd like to pray. My eighty-seven-year-old grandmother prayed one by one (in German) for each of her children and twelve grandchildren. I treasure that heritage of a praying grandmother. No matter what your family background, you can begin a heritage of prayer today that will impact future generations.

How about beginning now to pray for your children and grandchildren?

Response: *Lord, I praise You that You're my heavenly Father, my Rock, my shelter, and my fortress. I am sorry for the times I have neglected to pray. Thank You for Your faithfulness and everlasting love. Lord, You know the children I will raise. May they follow You all the days of their lives. May they shine like lights and lead many to know You. Please help me become a faithful prayer warrior for them and others. I commit now to pray for my children every day of my life. Bless my children, and may this heritage of prayer continue for all my future generations.*

A Heart for Husband and Friends

When a woman becomes a mother, it can change all of her relationships. A mother needs to continue a strong bond with her husband and friends. This week we'll hear from Kay, Leslie, Anne, Maria, and Debbie about how being a parent necessitated a commitment to their other relationships.

> ## A Heart for Husbands and Friends . . .
>
> Leaves and Cleaves—Kay
> Loves Her Husband—Leslie
> Uses the Instruction Manual—Anne
> Shares—Maria
> Accepts Help—Debbie

God is not only a loving father; in the person of Jesus Christ, He is also a husband. Christ's believers are His bride. That loving, committed, covenant relationship should be imitated in a husband and wife's relationship. This necessitates a commitment and a covenant.

Ephesians 5:31–32 states, "For this reason a man will leave his father and mother and be united to his wife, and the two will become one flesh. This is a profound mystery—but I am talking about Christ and the church."

Kay and I were roommates when I was in my early thirties, and we shared a house in Bellevue, Washington. We were both in long-distance relationships, except my fiancé lived on the other side of the *country* and hers was a widowed missionary with three kids on the other side of the *world*.

A Heart for Husband and Friends…
Leaves and Cleaves—Kay

When Kay became Mrs., she became an immediate step-mom to an eleven-year-old son, and nine- and six-year-old daughters. Mark and Kay followed the advice of their missions' pastor, and instead of returning to Croatia, they relocated to Azerbaijan—a new mission field for all five members of their family. This proved to be a wise move as it effectively leveled the playing field and caused all five to trust God and cleave to each other. After eighteen months, they returned to Croatia but finally settled in neighboring Bosnia.

Though Mark and Kay tried to have another child, God had another plan. Though it was "impossible" for foreigners to adopt, God opened the door for Mark and Kay to care for an abandoned three-month-old baby named Tomas. They petitioned to adopt and then waited, hoped, and prayed he could stay in their family. Days became weeks; weeks became months, and a year and a half passed. But suddenly, without warning, authorities stepped in and removed Tomas from the only father and mother he had ever known. Mark, Kay, and their children were devastated.

"Please, God, intervene," they prayed. The family clung to Psalms 37:39, "The salvation of the righteous comes from the LORD; he is their stronghold in time of trouble," and Psalms 3:8, "From the LORD comes deliverance." Believers around the world prayed. Each week Mark and Kay drove an hour and a half to the orphanage to see little Tomas; the parting was always tearful and agonizing. Why couldn't Mommy and Daddy stay? Why couldn't Mark and Kay take their little boy home? Where was God? They needed a miracle.

After nine months, the miracle happened. God chose to deliver Kay's family from a heavy grief. Mark and Kay, two *Americans*, were granted full adoption rights by the Bosnian government. God indeed was—and remains—their stronghold and salvation.

After over ten years of marriage and ministry on the mission field in war-torn Azerbaijan, Croatia, and Bosnia, what could Kay offer new mothers? A lot.

Bonding with her new children was accelerated by their move. They learned to depend on one another and forge family unity and harmony. Kay believes in the importance of stepping out together. "If you can't move, then go camping for a month!" she encourages. "One benefit in moving was that my identity was not, 'The woman who married Mark.'" Though it's drastic to move, Kay believes sometimes old identities have to be shattered in order for new identities to grow. "I did not feel as open, mature or fitted for my new role as I thought, and I became keenly aware of my lack. But I grew spiritually and grew into the role."

Heartwork

I've heard the joke, "The Bible says *two shall be one*, but WHICH one?" The idea is that the marriage bond creates a new flesh, a new covenant in Christ. Such a union can provide one of the strongest foundations for a child's growth. If you're not married, consider the person you might date. Is he worthy of your child's love? Will he be a godly father?

   1. Read the following scriptures about God's plan.

> *So the LORD God caused the man to fall into a deep sleep; and while he was sleeping, he took one of the man's ribs and closed up the place with flesh. Then the LORD God made a woman from the rib he had taken out of the man, and he brought her to the man.*
>
> *The man said, "This is now bone of my bones and flesh of my flesh; she shall be called 'woman,' for she was taken out of man." For this reason a man will leave his father and mother and be united to his wife, and they will become one flesh. (Genesis 2:21–24)*

The New Testament reaffirms that passage.

> *"But at the beginning of creation God 'made them male and female.' 'For this reason a man will leave his father and mother and be united to his wife, and the two will become one flesh.' So they are no longer two, but one. Therefore what God has joined together, let man not separate." (Mark 10:6–9)*

2. What does it really take to become one flesh?

_____

_____

_____

3. How can man separate "one flesh" (Mark 10:9)?

_____

_____

_____

4. What does it mean for a man to leave his father and mother? What are other things a spouse might need to leave in order to be fully committed to one flesh?

_____

_____

_____

5. In what ways do you need to cleave to your spouse and to God? (If you are not married, then think about this in the future tense.) How would this cleaving help strengthen your family?

_____

_____

_____

A solid, united marriage, one where both parties cleave to one another, gives security to your children. One mom wrote, "The best thing you can have going in your marriage as you enter motherhood, is a secure relationship with your spouse and the support of friends and family. Nothing matters more to kids than a loving environment." Children need the security of routines, personal attention, and the knowledge that both parents are committed to each other and the family.

6. The Bible gives us a beautiful example of leaving and cleaving in the story of Mary and Joseph. In the passages below, underline phrases or words where you see Mary and Joseph cleaving to one another and to God. Enjoy reading this model of commitment to God and to one another.

A Marriage Made in Heaven: Mary and Joseph

Matthew 1:18–24

This is how the birth of Jesus Christ came about: His mother Mary was pledged to be married to Joseph, but before they came together, she was found to be with child through the Holy Spirit. Because Joseph her husband was a righteous man and did not want to expose her to public disgrace, he had in mind to divorce her quietly.

But after he had considered this, an angel of the Lord appeared to him in a dream and said, "Joseph son of David, do not be afraid to take Mary home as your wife, because what is conceived in her is from the Holy Spirit.

She will give birth to a son, and you are to give him the name Jesus, because he will save his people from their sins."

All this took place to fulfill what the Lord had said through the prophet: "The virgin will be with child and will give birth to a son, and they will call him Immanuel"—which means, "God with us."

When Joseph woke up, he did what the angel of the Lord had commanded him and took Mary home as his wife.

Luke 2:1–7

In those days Caesar Augustus issued a decree that a census should be taken of the entire Roman world. (This was the first census that took place while Quirinius was governor of Syria.) And everyone went to his own town to register.

So Joseph also went up from the town of Nazareth in Galilee to Judea, to Bethlehem the town of David, because he belonged to the house and line of David. He went there to register with Mary, who was pledged to be married to him and was expecting a child. While they were there, the time came for the baby to be born, and she gave birth to her firstborn, a son. She wrapped him in cloths and placed him in a manger, because there was no room for them in the inn.

Matthew 2:13–23

When they had gone, an angel of the Lord appeared to Joseph in a dream. "Get up," he said, "take the child and his mother and escape to Egypt. Stay there until I tell you, for Herod is going to search for the child to kill him."

So he got up, took the child and his mother during the night and left for Egypt, where he stayed until the death of Herod. And so was fulfilled what the Lord had said through the prophet: "Out of Egypt I called my son."

When Herod realized that he had been outwitted by the Magi, he was furious, and he gave orders to kill all the boys in Bethlehem and its vicinity who were two years old and under, in accordance with the time he had learned from the Magi. Then what was said through the prophet Jeremiah was fulfilled: "A voice is heard in Ramah, weeping and great mourning, Rachel weeping for her children and refusing to be comforted, because they are no more."

After Herod died, an angel of the Lord appeared in a dream to Joseph in Egypt and said, "Get up, take the child and his mother and go to the land of Israel, for those who were trying to take the child's life are dead."

So he got up, took the child and his mother and went to the land of Israel. But when he heard that Archelaus was reigning in Judea in place of his father Herod, he was afraid to go there. Having been warned in a dream, he withdrew to the district of Galilee, and he went and lived in a town called Nazareth. So was fulfilled what was said through the prophets: "He will be called a Nazarene."

Luke 2:39–40

When Joseph and Mary had done everything required by the Law of the Lord, they returned to Galilee to their own town of Nazareth. And the child grew and became strong; he was filled with wisdom, and the grace of God was upon him.

Though Mary and Joseph were separated from home and family, they had each other and moved from place to place as God directed them. No matter where God leads you or what you do, cleave to your spouse. Your commitment to God and to your husband will bring your child a sense of security and stability.

Response: *Lord, help make us one flesh. May we love one another through You. Help my children know that You are the center of our home, and may they find security in this. Guide my words so they do not cause distress but instead bring unity and love. May we all cleave to You and to one another.*

Yesterday, you focused on the importance of cleaving, today let's look at the importance of loving your husband. Some of the most beautiful pieces of literature are found in Song of Songs.

> *Place me like a seal over your heart, like a seal on your arm; for love is as strong as death, its jealousy unyielding as the grave. It burns like blazing fire, like a mighty flame. (Song of Solomon 8:6)*

A Heart for Husband and Friends…
Loves her Husband—Leslie

Day Two

Leslie and Frank had been married for nine years when on Christmas Day, they received their best present ever in the form of little James McAlister or "Mac." Two years later, they were delighted by redheaded Jane Paige.

At a church gathering when Baby Paige was nine months old, Leslie explained how Paige was finally coming out of the colic stage and they were all now just falling in love with her. Leslie also expressed concern about spending all her attention on the new baby. Jean, a very wise member of her group and the most faith-filled woman Leslie had ever met, gave her a gift beyond measure.

> She explained that God had another plan for me as Paige's mother. She advised me to make a place for Christ at the center of my life, but that after Christ, my marriage/my husband was the center. And I needed to make that abun-

dantly clear to my children as they grew. She said, "without a strong marriage, your children will not have a good home to grow up in and not have good models to base their own adult lives on."

Jean stroked the back of Paige's neck and smiled at us both in the most lovely way and added that my children would one day leave home. If I have spent a lifetime with them at the center of my life, what will I do then? "Children will leave your home, but you and your husband will remain." —*Leslie*

Leslie knew she and Frank had a solid marriage and her children were gifts from God. Still, there was something true in Jean's words. Leslie had not been putting the same emphasis on her marriage. It was then she realized the best gift she could give Mac and Paige was a strong marriage.

Indeed, when a child feels part of a secure family, he can become his own little person. He doesn't have to worry about keeping two people together or making others happy, and he has a model for his future family as well.

You want to be a good Mommy? Respect your husband, and all the rest will fall into place! That is one of the most powerful and wonderful gifts you can give your child. It will leave a lasting legacy that will impact your family for generations to come. –Anne

Heartwork

Want some ideas on how to love your husband? Read on for fun and practical *heart*work!

1. Speak your husband's love language. Gary Chapman's book, *The Five Love Languages* encourages readers to discover their love language: Physical Touch, Receiving Gifts, Quality Time, Acts of Service, and Words of Affirmation. You can google a quiz to discover you and your husband's languages. If you have a minute, try it out: http://www.fivelovelanguages.com/ or try the thirty-second version {http://edified.org/myspace/lovelanguage}.

You may find it enlightening to speak your husband's love language.

2. Make dating your mate a priority.

Sometimes it takes creativity to keep the romance in a

"I belong to my lover, and his desire is for me." (Song of Solomon 7:10) marriage, but it's necessary! Find another couple to swap babysitting responsibilities. And then try making a game of your date. Give yourself a moderate budget and see how far you can stretch it with creativity and fun. Sign up for a fun class together. How about ballroom dancing? That will guarantee your date night. Hire a teenager for the duration of the class.

> "My lover is mine and I am his." (Song of Solomon 2:16)

As a child, I loved to see my parents dress up and go out. I enjoyed seeing my mom looking pretty and my dad taking her somewhere nice. You and your husband can model what a date should look like. Set a wonderful example for your children of what dating, marriage, romance, true love with commitment can look like.

Even though you might not think you need a date night, be proactive and schedule a time to focus on each other. You need to get away from diapers, dishes, and discipline. I've found that when we needed to vent at a restaurant, we had to speak gently. We had to be civilized and wait for our meal, and so we usually solved the problem by the time the bill came!

Besides your out-of-the-house dates, plan some "in-house" dates for when you've put the kids to bed. Watching TV does not count. Play backgammon, read a book aloud to one another, give each other back massages. Enjoy your spouse's company and companionship.

3. Read some enlightening material! There are numerous books that open the lines of communication and keep life in your marriage. Try reading a chapter a week and implementing the ideas. One title highlights the importance of a strong marriage: *Do Your Kids a Favor . . . Love Your Spouse* (Smiley and Smiley, Chicago: Moody Publishers, 2008). A few additional book suggestions follow:

BOOKS:

For Women Only: What You Need to Know about the Inner Lives of Men by Shaunti Feldhahn

Figure out some regular time when you can be with your husband to talk uninterrupted. Maybe it is just ten minutes before you both doze off or fifteen minutes right after dinner. Put little ones in a swing or a playpen for a bit; older kids can read or do a puzzle. My husband and I even now try to visit right after dinner or even the last part of dinner as our son is usually full before we are done. This connection is so important. Certainly aim for a weekly date if at all possible. *–Carrie*

(Sisters, OR: Multnomah Books, 2004)

For Men Only: A Straightforward Guide to the Inner Lives of Women by Shaunti and Jeff Feldhahn (Multnomah, 2006)

Love & Respect: The Love She Most Deserves; The Respect He Desperately Needs by Dr. Emerson Eggerichs (Nashville, TN: Thomas Nelson, 2004)

The Love List by Les and Leslie Parrott (or any book by this married couple) (Grand Rapids, MI: Zondervan, 2002).

4. Encourage your husband. Take on a new challenge for your marriage. Try saying only positive things *to* him and *about* him for one month. Nancy Leigh DeMoss' Revive our Hearts Ministry has a website where you can download a Thirty-Day Husband Encouragement Challenge. Not only is encouragement great for your spouse. Your kids will need it too, so practice now! Visit Revive Our Hearts at:

http://www.reviveourhearts.com/topics/downloads/index.php?id=9471

5. Make every day Valentine's Day. Be playful. The Word is exotic and a little erotic! How about this for an invitation note:

> *Come, my lover, let us go to the countryside, let us spend the night in the villages. Let us go early to the vineyards to see if the vines have budded, if their blossoms have opened, and if the pomegranates are in bloom—there I will give you my love. (Song of Solomon 7:11–12)*

What if your hubby found this note in his lunch?

> *How handsome you are, my lover! Oh, how charming! And our bed is verdant. (Song of Solomon 1:16)*

Or put your husband on a treasure hunt throughout your house; and *you* be the treasure he has to unwrap. One of my husband's fondest memories is of the time I left a trail of clothing leading from the front door all the way to the bedroom with a note on the door saying for him to match my articles of clothing with his. He loved the anticipation and thrill of the chase.

> "May your fountain be blessed, and may you rejoice in the wife of your youth. A loving doe, a graceful deer—may her breasts satisfy you always, may you ever be captivated by her love."
> (Proverbs 5:18–19)

Sound risqué? No. Besides being a mother, you're also a wife. Amidst all the diapers, dirt, and dentist appointments, remember you're a *woman* and your husband wants to see you that way!

Try taking turns reading excerpts from Song of Solomon. Whoever thought reading the Bible could be such fun?

She reads:

> *Like an apple tree among the trees of the forest is my lover among the young men. I delight to sit in his shade, and his fruit is sweet to my taste. He has taken me to the banquet hall, and his banner over me is love. Strengthen me with raisins, refresh me with apples, for I am faint with love. His left arm is under my head, and his right arm embraces me. (Song of Solomon 2:3–6)*

He reads:

> *Your neck is like the tower of David, built with elegance; on it hang a thousand shields, all of them shields of warriors. Your two breasts are like two fawns, like twin fawns of a gazelle that browse among the lilies. Until the day breaks and the shadows flee, I will go to the mountain of myrrh and to the hill of incense. All beautiful you are, my darling; there is no flaw in you. (Song of Solomon 4:4–7)*

> *You are a garden locked up, my sister, my bride; you are a spring enclosed, a sealed fountain. Your plants are an orchard of pomegranates with choice fruits, with henna and nard, nard and saffron, calamus and cinnamon, with every kind of incense tree, with myrrh and aloes and all the finest spices. (Song of Solomon 4:12–14)*

She reads:

> *Awake, north wind, and come, south wind! Blow on my garden, that its fragrance may spread abroad. Let my lover come into his garden and taste its choice fruits. (Song of Solomon 4:16)*

My lover is radiant and ruddy, outstanding among ten thousand. His head is purest gold; his hair is wavy and black as a raven. His eyes are like doves by the water streams, washed in milk, mounted like jewels. His cheeks are like beds of spice yielding perfume. His lips are like lilies dripping with myrrh. His arms are rods of gold set with chrysolite. His body is like polished ivory decorated with sapphires. His legs are pillars of marble set on bases of pure gold. His appearance is like Lebanon, choice as its cedars. His mouth is sweetness itself; he is altogether lovely. This is my lover, this my friend, O daughters of Jerusalem. (Song of Solomon 5:10–16)

"Love" is mentioned in 505 Bible verses, so it must be more than that mushy Valentine feeling, or the hot sensation that rushed through your veins when he first put his arm around you, or the absolutely overwhelming sensation when you first see your child, or when your family remembers your birthday with a big celebration. No, love is a decision and a choice. Make loving your spouse a priority and recognize its benefits.

Heartwork

Your family needs the foundation of a strong marriage. For ultimate strength, the Bible says two are better than one, and this verse implies there is strength in numbers.

There was a man all alone; he had neither son nor brother. There was no end to his toil, yet his eyes were not content with his wealth. "For whom am I toiling," he asked, "and why am I depriving myself of enjoyment?" This too is meaningless—a miserable business! Two are better than one, because they have a good return for their work: If one falls down, his friend can help him up. But pity the man who falls and has no one to help him up! Also, if two lie down together, they will keep warm. But how can one keep warm alone? Though one may be overpowered, two can defend themselves. A cord of three strands is not quickly broken. (Ecclesiastes 4:8–12)

1. Using the passage from Ecclesiastes 4, list the reasons why two are better than one.

_____

_____

_____

2. What is the third strand of a marriage?

_____

_____

_____

What picture can you keep in your house to remind you that ONE + ONE + GOD = THREE, a necessary formula for a strong marriage?

3. Using the rope analogy, how do marriages fray into separate pieces by going in separate directions? What are you doing in your marriage that may be fraying the bond?

_____

_____

_____

If your marriage is coming apart, look for help. In my brother's Bible study group, he discovered half of the couples were considering divorce. Though this was an intimate circle of friends; none were talking about their problems. Thus, none were able to help or share suggestions, and none were praying for each other. But in contrast, when one couple says, "We're having some issues and we're seeing a counselor," it can open the doors for others to share, be vulnerable, to help, and pray, and perhaps have the courage to see counselors as well. Many marriages could be saved with early intervention and counseling. A wise third party can often re-braid the cord of three. Instead of a marriage that barely survives, wouldn't you prefer a marriage that thrives?

4. If you and your husband trust in God and one another, how will this help bring a sense of security to your child's life? How will it help him to grow up knowing he has a secure rope to hang onto?

_____

_____

_____

> "Many waters cannot quench love; rivers cannot wash it away. If one were to give all the wealth of his house for love, it would be utterly scorned."
> (Song of Solomon 8:7)

Response: *Lord, as our family grows, help me remember to nurture my marriage. Teach me how to love my husband in ways that speak to him. Remind me to focus on his needs. Show me ways that I can respect and honor him. Help me not to be so overwhelmed by the joy and surprises of motherhood that I forget my child's father. May I understand loving my husband is a decision I make each day, not only on Valentine's Day.*

What if you were given directions on how to have greater peace and unity in your home, but the instructions were challenging? What if the directions involved humbling yourself?

When I get a set of instructions, I usually become frustrated with the diagrams and technical wording and cast aside the instructions to do it on my own. I may or may not be successful, but I'm usually frustrated. Sometimes we handle God's Word the same way.

My friend Anne handles the Bible with respect. Once Anne phoned just as my husband and I were arguing. I said I wasn't going back downstairs to finish the evening with my husband, but she said I needed to get off the phone and resolve things right then. She spoke the truth in love, and my husband has encouraged our friendship ever since! Today's lesson is a little longer than the rest—and a little tougher, so take heart and prepare a cup of tea, and sit down to take in the Word.

May the God who gives endurance and encouragement give you a spirit of unity among yourselves as you follow Christ Jesus, so that with one heart and mouth you may glorify the God and Father of our Lord Jesus Christ. (Romans 15:5–6)

Anne's pursuit of God's Word began when her first child was born and has continued through every stage of her three children's growth. She learned the Bible is a great instruction manual, but the coursework is often challenging.

Respecting Husbands 101

Each one of you also must love his wife as he loves himself, and the wife must respect her husband. (Ephesians 5:33)

I looked at my husband Scot and apologized for mucking it up so bad with my, "You do fifty percent of the work and I'll do fifty percent and we'll be fine." We weren't fine. It was a disaster. When I started to implement the truth of God's Word and His plan for my marriage, I saw amazing fruit.

God does not tell us to love our husbands but to respect them, as that is how they feel loved. For years I tried to love my husband the way I wanted to be loved, and he was not feeling it. That is not what he needed from me; God said he needed my respect. I believe the very best gift I could ever give my children is to respect their daddy. It sets the entire foundation for our family. If I do not respect my husband, our family foundation is flawed, and there is no security and peace for any of us.

When I show respect to my husband, I don't have to worry about any of my needs being met. I am loved and treated like a queen by the Lord, through my husband. As God promises, "all our needs will be met according to His riches in Christ Jesus." Trust God that in being obedient to

His word you will be blessed. —*Anne*

Anne learned that her faith had an umbrella policy.

When our children were younger, God gave me this picture to open an umbrella over them and explain that when they obey God and Mom and Dad, they are safe and protected and under God's covering like the umbrella. But when they disobey, they walk away from the protection. When I was going through a time of frustration with my husband, I realized that my husband is *my* umbrella of protection. God works through him and if I step out from under that, then I choose to walk away from God's protection for me.

It is so important to teach our children to respect and obey the authority God places in their lives. We must train our children so when they grow into adults, they will not choose to rebel and walk away from God's protection. We must teach by example. Are we walking under God's protection? —*Anne*

Teaching Her Children to Respect 201

Children, obey your parents in everything, for this pleases the Lord. (Colossians 3:20)

As Anne followed the instruction manual in her marriage, she also looked to it for parenting advice.

I went back to God's word for guidance; after all, He created my children and the Bible was His instruction manual for how to live here on earth. The verses that were first and foremost in instructing my children were, "Train a child in the way he should go, and when he is old he will not turn from it'" (Proverbs 22:6). And "Children, obey your parents in the Lord for this is right" (Ephesians 6:1). These verses framed the parameters in how we would raise our children. —*Anne*

> "My son, keep your father's commands and do not forsake your mother's teaching. Bind them upon your heart forever; fasten them around your neck. When you walk, they will guide you; when you sleep, they will watch over you; when you awake, they will speak to you." (Proverbs 6:20–22)

Anne and Scot have a son, two daughters, and a baby on the way. As a family, they've had their struggles, but God has seen them through.

Six years ago I struggled with a debilitating autoimmune disease that affected the neurons of my brain. For two years I was unable to care for my children well. Since there were times I couldn't get out of bed, my elementary-aged children looked after one another, did their laundry, picked up after themselves, and prepared meals. At an early age Scot and I had taught them to obey immediately and with a proper attitude. Though God has healed me of that incurable disease, he used those two years to prepare my children in many ways for the life that lies ahead of them.

God's Word has become our family's instruction Fmanual and has been a huge blessing in forming our family legacy. It is not about us alone or our children but our children's children and future generations and the impact that our family will have on God's kingdom. —*Anne*

> "But from everlasting to everlasting the LORD's love is with those who fear him, and his righteousness with their children's children—with those who keep his covenant and remember to obey his precepts." (Psalms 103:17–18)

Because Anne recognizes the Bible as her "instruction manual," she loves to study it. Anne applies God's Word and claims His promises daily. All treasures of wisdom she would share with you come straight from the Word of God.

I can tell you that I love the journey of being a parent. I have been blessed beyond measure by the Word of God! It is the best parenting manual ever written. It has brought into the life of my family a peace and certainty of where we will spend eternity and a plan on how we are to walk out our lives here on earth including the teen years fast approaching. How can you prepare for motherhood? Get into the Word of God! —*Anne*

Ephesians 4:3 says, "Make every effort to keep the unity of the Spirit through the bond of peace."

The Word of God encourages us to love one another and to live at peace. Today's heartwork should help us understand how that can be accomplished.

Heartwork

Our heartwork begins with the goal of peace in the body of Christ and in the home.

1. First read what could be your family's goal—even framed to remind your family of peace and unity. Underline words you'd love to see implemented in your home.

> *Let the peace of Christ rule in your hearts, since as members of one body you were called to peace. And be thankful. Let the word of Christ dwell in you richly as you teach and admonish one another with all wisdom, and as you sing psalms, hymns and spiritual songs with gratitude in your hearts to God. And whatever you do, whether in word or deed, do it all in the name of the Lord Jesus, giving thanks to God the Father through him. (Colossians 3:15–17)*

What follows this delightful goal are lessons from the greatest instruction manual to help you accomplish it. The left column continues in Colossians, and the middle and right columns are other passages Paul wrote on the subject.

Further Instructions from the Manual

1. Connect the verses that are similar in content.
2. Underline *who* Paul is addressing in each verse. There's something for everybody!

Colossians 3	**Ephesians 5**	**Ephesians 6**
Colossians <u>3:18</u> Wives, submit to your husbands, as is fitting in the Lord.	Ephesians <u>5:21</u> Submit to one another out of reverence for Christ.	Ephesians <u>6:1</u> Children, obey your parents in the Lord, for this is right.
Colossians <u>3:19</u> Husbands, love your wives and do not be harsh with them.	Ephesians <u>5:22</u> Wives, submit to your husbands as to the Lord.	Ephesians <u>6:2</u> "Honor your father and mother"—which is the first commandment with a promise."
Colossians <u>3:20</u> Children, obey your parents in everything, for this pleases the Lord.	Ephesians <u>5:25</u> Husbands, love your wives, just as Christ loved the church and gave himself up for her.	Ephesians <u>6:3</u> "that it may go well with you and that you may enjoy long life on the earth."
	Ephesians <u>5:33</u> However, each one of you also must love his wife as he loves himself, and the wife must respect her husband.	

3. What would a home look like where everybody respected and honored God as well as one another? How would you feel living in such a family environment?

_____

_____

_____

4. How could the way you treat your husband affect how your children honor and obey their father? Or how they honor and obey you?

_____

_____

_____

> "Wives, in the same way be submissive to your husbands so that, if any of them do not believe the word, they may be won over without words by the behavior of their wives, when they see the purity and reverence of your lives." (1 Peter 3:1–2)

5. In what ways could the way *you* treat your husband affect how your children honor and obey *God?*

_____

_____

_____

6. There are plenty of ways to respect your husband. Ask your husband how you are doing in showing respect for him in the following areas:

His role, responsibilities, time, efforts, thoughts, concerns, opinions, questions, career, suggestions, leadership, parenting

What can you do *today* to begin honoring and respecting your husband?

_____

_____

_____

7. In what ways do you struggle with the word "submit"? Can you take that challenge to the Lord and journal a prayer below?

_____

_____

_____

_____

8. Using the above verses addressed to children, list reasons for them to honor and obey their parents. What promise follows?

_____

_____

_____

Throughout the Old Testament, we find the command to honor your father and mother. It's the first commandment with a promise (Exodus 20:12; Leviticus 19:3; Deuteronomy 5:16). Jesus repeats it in the New Testament (Matthew 15:4; 19:19; Mark 10:19; Luke 18:20). It must be important: commands have a reason, a promise, or a plan.

> "This is how we know what love is: Jesus Christ laid down his life for us. And we ought to lay down our lives for our brothers."
> (1 John 3:16)

The Ephesians 5 passage in the chart we discussed earlier goes on in much more depth as a beautiful description of Jesus' love. Jesus loved the church sacrificially. Paul challenged husbands to love their wives just as Jesus loved the church. The passage continues with this analogy and discusses the *mystery* of marriage, concluding with mutual love and respect.

📖 9. Before you read the passage, ask God to nudge you in any way you need nudging and to help you understand and apply the passage. Underline anything you find interesting.

For the husband is the head of the wife as Christ is the head of the church, his body, of which he is the Savior. Now as the church submits to Christ, so also wives should submit to their husbands in everything.

Husbands, love your wives, just as Christ loved the church and gave himself up for her to make her holy, cleansing her by the washing with water through the word, and to present her to himself as a radiant church, without stain or wrinkle or any other blemish, but holy and blameless. In this same way, husbands ought to love their wives as their own bodies. He who loves his wife loves himself. After all, no one ever hated his own body, but he

> "Listen, my son, to your father's instruction and do not forsake your mother's teaching. They will be a garland to grace your head and a chain to adorn your neck." (Proverbs 1:8–9)

feeds and cares for it, just as Christ does the church—for we are members of his body. "For this reason a man will leave his father and mother and be united to his wife, and the two will become one flesh." This is a profound mystery—but I am talking about Christ and the church. However, each one of you also must love his wife as he loves himself, and the wife must respect her husband. (Ephesians 5:23–33)

Paul continues with similar words in Colossians 3 and Ephesians 6. When he talks about obedience, he asks his listeners to obey with a sincere heart, wholeheartedly as if serving the Lord, not men, and to do the will of God from their hearts. And though the comments are directed to slaves, Paul concludes, "Because you know that the Lord will reward everyone for whatever good he does, whether he is slave or free" (Ephesians 6:8–9). Our Lord's reward should be reason enough for us to serve one another.

Bottom line? You need a game plan for how your household will function. You have an instruction manual, and you can choose to follow it or go your own way. Your attitude and willingness to respect God's Word will have a direct affect on how your children honor and respect others and His Word.

10. Perhaps your family needs to practice honoring and respecting one another. Do you have a family motto or verse? Maybe selecting a family verse or motto would help. Write a verse or motto below.

_____

_____

_____

But if serving the LORD seems undesirable to you, then choose for yourselves this day whom you will serve, whether the gods your forefathers served beyond the River, or the gods of the Amorites, in whose land you are living. But as for me and my household, we will serve the LORD." (Joshua 24:15)

Response: *Lord, as for me and my house, we will serve You. Since serving You means honoring and respecting my husband,* *then give me the strength and wisdom to do just that. Since serving You means teaching my children to honor You, and my husband and me, then help me to set a proper role model for my children. Help me to be strong in You, mighty in Your power. Help our home to be filled with peace. Bless us as we serve You wholeheartedly.*

What a privilege to talk to God and to your husband. Still, the friendships of other women also benefit you in mothering. At this shower of wisdom, a repeated piece of advice from women has been that moms need the counsel of other mothers, and to gather together for wisdom and support. The Bible supports this kind of fellowship. Read how it affected one of my dear friends.

"As iron sharpens iron, so one man sharpens another." (Proverbs 27:17)

A Heart for Husband and Friends…
Shares—Maria

"What a roller coaster ride it has been!" Maria exclaimed. I could only imagine. Maria is the mother of four boys! What would a dynamic, energetic woman like Maria say about preparing for *that*?

> I remember one day when I had just had it with the baby. I was working part-time and staying home the other days. As a first-time mom, I felt frustrated with all the expectations. You think the dad will understand you've been with the baby all day, your hormones are raging, and you're lonely and you need someone to talk to. Once when Krag came home late from work, I threw a shoe at him! —*Maria*

What Maria wished she had known before she began parenting was that Moms need fellowship, and more specifically, the wisdom of older moms. Maria needed to talk to someone who could understand her feelings.

Krag and Maria's three sons were five, three, and eleven months when Maria gave birth to Natalie Maria. Natalie and their youngest son were so close in age, they were on track to enter kindergarten together. But they never did. When Natalie was but four months old, she died of Sudden Infant Death Syndrome (SIDS). Devastated, the family clung to the verse carved on Natalie's tombstone, "All the days ordained for me were written in your book before one of them came to be" (Psalms 139:16).

After Natalie's death, Kathleen, a mother of seven sons, became Maria's mentor. Lisa, a mother of four, also counseled her for several hours a day. They were older parents—unafraid of being transparent, they had walked the path before her and could advise and encourage her.

> "He who walks with the wise grows wise."
> (Proverbs 13:20)

Maria has learned to open up to others, and shares her parenting struggles. She lets others know when times are difficult. Women are drawn to her because of her enthusiasm for life and her acceptance that everything isn't perfect. She advises sharing your joys and sorrows because this will lighten your load. "A lot of people are afraid to share and admit they're not perfect—especially moms," Maria points out. But Maria recognizes moms need to share more than others.

This kind of fellowship involves transparent, nurturing relationships with women who are years ahead in parenting. Like iron sharpening iron, new mothers need wise counselors to sharpen them.

Too often you may be tempted to surround yourself with parents with kids of similar ages, but what you need are older moms who reveal the bigger picture. You'll need to know your toddler will not go to college in diapers, your third-grader may one day *choose* to read a book, and your pre-teenage daughters' outbursts are hormonally based and normal, or your adolescent son will begin to distance himself from you. You need someone older and wiser to point out the mile markers on the marathon of parenting.

After eighteen years of marriage and the arrival of a fourth son, Maria now has more perspective on the seasons of parenting. She loves having friends who now walk where she's walked, and she enjoys listening to those who are ahead of her on the journey. God has blessed her with friends and the fellowship of moms in many stages of parenting.

Heartwork

Consider Mary and Elizabeth in the Bible, two expectant moms enjoying three months of companionship. They shared the story of God's revelation in their lives and looked forward to what God had planned for them and their children. Mary must have enjoyed having an older woman to share with, and Elizabeth must have appreciated her relative's youthful enthusiasm. You, too, need godly mentors and friends who help you in your journey of faith. Gathering together with other believers encourages prayer, builds your faith, teaches you how to love your family, and builds community.

Encourages Prayer

Men and women believers in the early church all joined together constantly in prayer (Acts 1:14–15). The church provides a wonderful place for this kind of unity, but small Bible study groups and play dates can add further fellowship. Sometimes when you feel you're struggling in your faith, it's helpful to share with a fellow Christian.

1. What does the following "each other" scripture say you should do besides confess your sins? "Therefore confess your sins to each other and pray for each other so at you may be healed. The prayer of a righteous man is powerful and effective" (James 5:16).

_____   _____

_____   _____

_____

While we're on the subject of prayer and sharing, I'll insert this caution: groups that become gossipy instead of glorifying to God, more whiney than winsome, and bash husbands instead of building them up, are not beneficial. The Bible repeatedly warns against women who do that (Proverbs 11:13; 16:28; 18:8; 20:19; 25:24; 26:20; 27:15; 2 Corinthians 12:20).

Instead of idle chatter, remember the big *whatever* verse from Philippians 4:8 (emphasis added):

Whatever!

Whatever is true, whatever is noble, whatever is right, whatever is pure, whatever is lovely, whatever is admirable—if anything is excellent or praiseworthy—think about such things.

Builds Faith

I was in a Bible study where we learned that the sign language for FAITH is to point to your head for "know" and then put one fist on top of another like rock solid faith for "hold." I love that we are *holding* onto what we *think*. When we gather together in Christ, we encourage one another in our faith. "Now faith is being sure of what we hope for and certain of what we do not see" (Hebrews 11:1).

You will not always see God working in your own life, but it will encourage you to see what He's doing in others around you. And sometimes they will see with greater perspective what He's accomplishing in you. Sometimes you need reminding that just because you cannot *see* what He's doing, you need to keep the faith, because He is at work in your life!

2. Hebrews 10:19–22 explains that since Jesus gave His life as a blood sacrifice for our sin, you can draw near to God and you have been cleansed from all sin. The passage goes on to give some specifics for when you gather together with others. What four things do verses 23–25 say you need to do?

_____

_____

_____

Let us hold unswervingly to the hope we profess, for he who promised is faithful. And let us consider how we may spur one another on toward love and good deeds. Let us not give up meeting together, as some are in the habit of doing, but let us encourage one another—and all the more as you see the Day approaching.

Teaches How to Love

3. Some organizations such as Mothers of Preschoolers have "Titus 2" women who help the younger women. Using the chart below, what does Titus 2 say is the responsibility of the older women, and what are the needs of the younger women?

_____

_____

_____

You must teach what is in accord with sound doctrine. Teach the older men to be temperate, worthy of respect, self-controlled, and sound in faith, in love and in endurance.

Likewise, teach the older women to be reverent in the way they live, not to be slanderers or addicted to much wine, but to teach what is good. Then they can train the younger women to love their husbands and children, to be self-controlled and pure, to be busy at home, to be kind, and to be subject to their husbands, so that no one will malign the word of God. (Titus 2:1–5)

Older Women's Responsibilities	Younger Women's Needs

Builds Community

And finally, as part of a body of believers, you have a function (1 Corinthians 12:4–31; Ephesians 4:11–13). Romans 12 gives many instructions on how to function together in harmony.

> As we struggle with the teenage years, I often think back to when I was a teen and how awkward those years were. I try to be patient and firm, but I frequently seek advice from wise mothers who have raised teenagers. —Becky

> Love must be sincere. Hate what is evil; cling to what is good. Be devoted to one another in brotherly love. Honor one another above yourselves. Never be lacking in zeal, but keep your spiritual fervor, serving the Lord. Be joyful in hope, patient in affliction, faithful in prayer. Share with God's people who are in need. Practice hospitality.
>
> Bless those who persecute you; bless and do not curse. Rejoice with those who rejoice; mourn with those who mourn. Live in harmony with one another. Do not be proud, but be willing to associate with people of low position. Do not be conceited.
>
> Do not repay anyone evil for evil. Be careful to do what is right in the eyes of everybody. If it is possible, as far as it depends on you, live at peace with everyone. (Romans 12:9–18)

4. According to verse 10, how are you to treat others?

_____

_____

_____

5. What are some practical ways to demonstrate verse 13 when you are in a group?

_____

_____

_____

6. How could verse 15 be a part of a group setting?

_____

_____

_____

From this study, you've learned about your need for a relationship with God and your husband. But you've also seen the need for wisdom from Christian sisters. Begin or continue praying for a group of godly Christian women with whom to share. Look for a mentor who would be a good role model as you parent. What steps are you taking to meet with other women or to reach out and encourage other moms? How will having a group of godly friends effect your mothering now and in years to come?

7. Journal below your needs for friendship. Pray specifically about these needs.

_____

_____

_____

Response: *Lord, help me to find Christian moms who will share biblical wisdom with me. Help me understand that when I am weak, You are strong. Let me be vulnerable and transparent with others so they can point me to You. Help me to be faithful in prayer for my children and for my parenting.*

At some point in your parenting, you will need the help of friends. This help may be the hands of Christ reaching out. You may be the type of mom who prefers to serve rather than be served, but there will be times your family will benefit if you allow others to assist. Will you accept your friends' helpful hands?

A Heart for Husband and Friends…
Accepts Help—Debbie

"My grace is sufficient for you, for my power is made perfect in weakness." Therefore I will boast all the more gladly about my weaknesses, so that Christ's power may rest on me. That is why, for Christ's sake, I delight in

weaknesses, in insults, in hardships, in persecutions, in difficulties. For when I am weak, then I am strong. (2 Corinthians 12:9–10)

Debbie and Keith's two daughters were born three years apart. Their family was busy and active, and their lives were full. Debbie taught school, and Keith served as an ER doctor. Both were involved in their daughters elementary school activities. Still, they felt called to adopt a child from Ethiopia.

Their daughters, Betsy and Kristin, were excited about the opportunity; Keith and Debbie felt cautious. Some African children had serious health issues and even terminal illnesses. Debbie and Keith wanted to protect the girls from loss, and so limited their choices to what they felt their family could handle. They chose Frew, a boy with Hepatitis B, who was the same age as 6-year-old Kristin.

Kristin and Betsy helped prepare their brother's room, carefully chose his first teddy bear, and helped stitch a blankie. Then Keith flew from Anchorage, Alaska, to Ethiopia to adopt the newest member of the Winkle family.

But a year later they were hit with the possibility of terminal illness. Debbie had suffered from persistent headaches, but as an athlete, she always toughed things out, never asking for help. She never pursued medical treatment, but as the family prepared to go to Disney World, the frequency and intensity of the pain increased, necessitating an MRI.

As Debbie delivered the brain scan to her doctor, she opened up the x-ray and looked at the image. Though not the ER doctor of the family, she could tell there was something terribly wrong with the picture. Debbie kept silent about the results, but once in Disney World, Debbie kept wondering if all the health warning signs near the rides were meant for her. She kept asking others to take a "family" picture, wondering if this occasion might be one of their last together. Would Frew lose yet another mother? Would Keith, with his crazy ER schedule, have to raise their three children alone?

When they returned to Anchorage, Debbie immediately flew to Seattle for surgery to remove a large tumor. Her hearing in one ear was lost, and the nerves on one side of her face were cut, giving her the appearance of a stroke victim at the age of thirty-nine. No longer able to blink, a weighted chip was added to her eyelid to help it close. The good news was the tumor was not malignant and she would live; unfortunately, the recovery would take not days or weeks, but *months* or even *years*.

Debbie could no longer enjoy the title of "super mom." She wanted to be the one to help, not the one needing it. But now she needed assistance with everything: driving, cooking, cleaning, shopping, laundry, and carpooling. Where was the former Debbie who could help the kids with their homework and play at the park? Instead her friends stepped in to take the kids out for fun activities and a good time. Her mom flew to Alaska to help run the household.

After a slow recovery, the firsts were an almost overwhelming challenge: loading and unloading the dishwasher and dryer, driving the car. Finally one day her mother returned to Seattle and left her alone to be Mom again. Because of the surgery, Debbie learned to rely solely on God and the people around her. She exchanged self-confidence and independence for humility and a willingness to be helped.

I can relate on a much smaller level. When we moved to an unfamiliar area, I wore my daughters on my hips everywhere I went, never seeking help from others. I thought I could do it all. But that didn't make me a better mom, and it didn't allow others to get to know me by helping out. You see, when friends ask friends for help, they show a level of trust, believing the friendship is strong enough and will deepen through the experience.

> "Let no debt remain outstanding, except the continuing debt to love one another, for he who loves his fellow man has fulfilled the law."
>
> (Romans 13:8)

One of my longtime friends avoided me for months because she was so overwhelmed by her colicky baby. I felt a loss and hurt because she didn't trust our friendship to last through the screaming and tears. When later she herself had a health emergency, I felt honored she considered me a trusted enough friend to watch her kids overnight.

Trust God with your problems. Go to Him with your burdens, and you'll become aware of how keenly He understands your needs. And ask for help from others. There's nothing wrong with reaching out to somebody you trust. Your humble acceptance of help allows others to experience the joy of serving. And if you don't feel *you* need help, maybe you need to look out for a friend who does!

> "Carry each other's burdens, and in this way you will fulfill the law of Christ." (Galatians 6:2)

Heartwork

1. When you have a need, remember God loves you and is trustworthy. You can pray to Him for direction.

Trust in the LORD with all your heart and lean not on your own understanding; in all your ways acknowledge him, and he will make your paths straight. (Proverbs 3:5–6)

*Let the morning bring me word of your unfailing love, for I have **put my trust** in you. Show me the way I should go, for to you I lift up my soul. (Psalms 143:8 [emphasis added])*

In your prayers, ask God to provide good friends who are trustworthy. The counsel of a friend is a wonderful gift. But it necessitates wisdom. Choose godly friends with godly wisdom. "Perfume and incense bring joy to the heart, and the pleasantness of one's **friend** springs from his earnest counsel" (Proverbs 27:9 [emphasis added]).

2. If you have good friends, don't be afraid to ask for help. Sometimes as moms, we have trouble asking for help or accepting help from others. What keeps you from asking for help?

_____

_____

_____

_____

The New Testament woman, who bled for years, reached out and touched Jesus. The Canaanite mother with a suffering child begged for help from the Lord. The paralyzed man beside the pool in Bethesda needed someone to put him in the waters when the pool was stirred. The centurion found Jesus and asked Him to heal His son. Remember the Sunday school story about the paralytic who could not get into the house where Jesus was teaching to be healed? His friends broke a hole in the roof and lowered him down.

Over and over, people ask for help from God. Over and over, people need the assistance of friends. These are the friends who love at all times.

3. Proverbs 17:17 says, "A **friend** loves at all times, and a brother is born for adversity" (emphasis added). In what ways do you need to be a friend who loves at all times? How can you become more aware of your friends' needs? Think of a specific person and kind deed.

_____

_____

_____

_____

4. What makes you try to be super mom? How can you show a friend that you trust her enough to be willing to ask for help?

_____

_____

_____

_____

5. Read today's opening verse again. What have you learned from it you can put into practice?

_____

_____

_____

_____

Serving and comforting others are ways to put your faith into action. It's a privilege to comfort in the way God has comforted you.

Praise be to the God and Father of our Lord Jesus Christ, the Father of compassion and the God of all comfort, who comforts us in all our troubles, so that we can comfort those in any trouble with the comfort we ourselves have received from God. (2 Corinthians 1:3–4)

Response: Lord, I long to put my trust in You. Bring friends into my life who are trustworthy, kind, gentle, and godly counselors. When I need help, give me the strength and humility to ask for it. For when I am weak, then You are strong in me.

A Changed Heart

Motherhood changes your heart like no other experience. With your first child, you see the world in a fresh new way. This week we'll focus on how God can change your heart through motherhood. We'll hear stories from Sherrill, Carrie, Sandra, Jen, and Tina about how God healed their hearts and how that caused a hunger to change.

A Changed Heart . . .

Is Reborn—Sherrill
Is Forgiven—Carrie
Forgives—Sandra
Is a Heart of No Compare—Jen
Gets a Fresh Start in the Word—Tina

Not every pregnancy is planned. Not every mother is prepared. What if expecting was unexpected? What happens when the big announcement isn't met with joy?

Praise be to the God and Father of our Lord Jesus Christ! In His great mercy He has given us new birth into a living hope through the resurrection of Jesus Christ from the dead. (1 Peter 1:3)

A Changed Heart... Is Reborn—Sherrill   *Day One*

When twenty-nine-year-old Sherrill became pregnant, she was single and had just lost her job. How could she tell her parents? With dread, she broke the news.

Her parents were disappointed. But though Sherrill feared disownment, her father handed her the book *Born Again*, Chuck Colson's account of his illegal involvement in Watergate and his subsequent jail term. Sherrill's father wanted her to see an example of how God gave hope and promise to someone who made a potentially life-shattering choice. He wanted to help her understand that challenges can present choices to change.

Sherrill faced a major turning point in her life. Would she live the faith she professed or continue on a negative path? When she read about the Israelites wandering in the desert constantly rebelling and repenting, she used to wonder, "How could they forget God's mercy over and over again?" Then she recognized the same pattern in her life. "My unplanned pregnancy was sort of the culmination of my rebel-sin-repent-obey cycle. I was always desperately seeking love, acceptance, and validation. Something deep inside made me think and feel I was not worthy of love."

That emptiness needed to be filled with God. Both she and her child needed Him. Not every mother has an earthly father to raise her child, and that was Sherrill's case. But every mother has a heavenly Father who loves her child even more than she does. Could Sherrill accept God's love and cross over to where God wanted her to be? Finally, she came to the place of total surrender and cried out, "God, I know you can create beauty out of any situation. I'm sorry I've made such a mess, but here it is. Do whatever you will with my life. If I never marry, I will trust you to be my husband and a father to my child."

God showed His love and grace through a baby shower hosted by her parents' Sunday school class. Women she had never met showered her with love, support, and an outpouring of God's mercy and grace, leading to Sherrill's spiritual transformation. Sherrill had new hope, and she was "born again" just as the child would be born from her. And because of this unborn child, Sherrill stopped making self-destructive choices and began making positive choices for herself and her baby.

Surprisingly, Sherrill also had the privilege of **meeting** Charles Colson, the author of *Born Again*, who later wrote her:

> I must say having met you now, however, that I rejoice all the more in what God is doing in your life. You have a

radiance about you that comes from Christ. I am sure He is guiding your steps and I am both humbled and grateful that my books have played a role in that. . . . I will pray that the Lord will keep His hand on you, bring you through these difficult periods, making you stronger than ever. As you know from reading my book, it is through adversity that we are strengthened. I look back on my own life and realize that I gained little from all the successes and achievements; it was in the brokenness that God did His greatest work.

Indeed, it was in Sherrill's brokenness that God did His greatest work. At the beginning of the new year and her new understanding in Christ, God blessed Sherrill with a beautiful son whom she named Jordan Matthew, meaning "*Crossing over, Gift from God.*" Her son bears the name of the river in which Jesus was baptized (Matthew 3:13) and where many followers repented of their sins and were baptized (Mark 1:5). In the Old Testament, crossing over the Jordan meant entering the Promised Land. "You are about to cross the **Jordan** to enter and take possession of the land the LORD your God is giving you" (Deuteronomy 11:31). Sherrill explained, "Getting pregnant brought me to my knees in repentance and surrender. After all the years of wandering in the wilderness, I had to cross the Jordan (my pregnancy) to enter the Promised Land where God could finally bless me as He had always wanted to."

With forty pounds of pregnancy weight and a five-month-old baby, Sherrill didn't feel like dating material, but nevertheless, she met Norm. God in His goodness and mercy blessed Jordan with an earthly father who would love them like their heavenly Father. And so, a year and a half later, Norm and Sherrill married and later added a daughter to their family. God has been faithful in the lives of Norm, Sherrill, Jordan, and Sara. Indeed, their lives have been "born again" as they serve God.

> I really wondered if God would be willing to use me in ministry. Or was I damaged goods and never to have a place to serve Him? In time I realized that, maybe more because of my sin rather than in spite of it, God would use me, because He had a plan to bring glory to Him. —*Sherrill*

Some may cringe at the term "born again." Some may frown in confusion because it doesn't make sense to them. For some it sounds "Christianese." However, Jesus used this *maternal* term to signify the moment a non-believer becomes a Christian, and that makes this term all the more beautiful.

The familiar term "born again" appears in the middle of a fascinating story about a Pharisee. Nicodemus was a man who wanted to follow all the rules to the letter of the law. Though the other Jewish leaders denounced Jesus as the Messiah, Nicodemus sought Jesus out in secret. Jesus told Nicodemus that one must be "born again" to inherit the kingdom of God. As Nicodemus was thinking of literal childbirth, he queried Jesus, "How can a **man** be **born again**?"

Jesus' response is perhaps one of the most familiar passages in scripture. His answer is sometimes displayed as background wallpaper at football games, shouted from street corners, and printed on evangelical tracts. Unfortunately, many read it without really thinking about it. What is the setting for His Word from John 3:16? It's in the same passage as the phrase "born again." Put down your pencil and enjoy reading these scriptures as if for the first time.

John 3:1–18 (emphasis added)

Now there was a man of the Pharisees named Nicodemus, a member of the Jewish ruling council. He came to Jesus at night and said, "Rabbi, we know you are a teacher who has come from God. For no one could perform the miraculous signs you are doing if God were not with him."

*In reply Jesus declared, "I tell you the truth, no one can see the kingdom of God unless he is **born again**."*

"How can a man be born when he is old?" Nicodemus asked. "Surely he cannot enter a second time into his mother's womb to be born!"

Jesus answered, "I tell you the truth, no one can enter the kingdom of God unless he is born of water and the Spirit. Flesh gives birth to flesh, but the Spirit gives birth to spirit. You should not be surprised at my saying, 'You *must be **born again**.' The wind blows wherever it pleases. You hear its sound, but you cannot tell where it comes from or where it is going. So it is with everyone born of the Spirit."*

"How can this be?" Nicodemus asked.

"You are Israel's teacher," said Jesus, "and do you not understand these things? I tell you the truth, we speak of what we know, and we testify to what we have seen, but still you people do not accept our testimony. I have spoken to you of earthly things and you do not believe; how then will you believe if I speak of heavenly things? No one has ever gone into heaven except the one who came from heaven—the Son of Man. Just as Moses lifted up the snake in the desert, so the Son of Man must be lifted up, that everyone who believes in him may have eternal life.

For God so loved the world that he gave his one and only Son, that whoever believes in him shall not perish but have eternal life. *For God did not send his Son into the world to condemn the world, but to save the world through him. Whoever believes in him is not condemned, but whoever does not believe stands condemned already because he has not believed in the name of God's one and only Son.*

📖 1. Re-read John 3:16–18 but insert your name:

"For God so loved _____ that he gave _____his one and only Son, that if _____ believe in him, _____shall not perish but have eternal life. For God did not send his Son into the world to condemn _____, but to save _____through him. If _____believes in him _____is not condemned, but if _____does not believe _____stands condemned already because _____has not believed in the name of God's one and only Son.

The Son of Man was lifted up to die on the cross. He rose again that those who believe might live with Him forever. He offers salvation. If you've never accepted Jesus into your life, what's stopping you from making this commitment? To be "born again" means to pray a prayer similar to this:

Lord Jesus,

I have made many wrong choices in my life, but I want to make the right choice now. And that choice is YOU. I believe in You. I believe You were born on earth to bring salvation to all who believe in You. I believe You took the punishment for my sins when You died on the cross. Please forgive me for my sins and make me whiter than snow. I rejoice that You rose again and I am asking You to live in my heart and guide my life from this point forward. I surrender my life to You. I love You, Jesus. In Your precious and Holy name. Amen.

If you made a choice to follow Christ, please write the date below. If you, like Sherrill, made a recommitment of your faith, write that recommitment and date below.

_____

You are a new creation in Him! "*The old has gone, the new has come!*" (2 Corinthians 5:16–21)

2. Sherrill's story testifies to the grace of God. **G**od's **R**iches **A**t **C**hrist's **E**xpense. How can your story tell of God's grace? How could your life be used for His glory?

_____

_____

_____

"However, I consider my life worth nothing to me, if only I may finish the race and complete the task the Lord Jesus has given me—the task of testifying to the gospel of God's grace." (Acts 20:24, emphasis added)

3. In what ways is God using your role as a mother to shape your life and your faith?

_____

_____

_____

4. How does having a child in your home change your relationship with Christ? And in what ways does the addition of your child remind you that you are *born again* into the kingdom of God?

_____

_____

_____

5. How can you prepare your child to know Jesus and help him choose to follow Christ?

_____

_____

_____

Response: *Lord, thank You for giving me the privilege of being born again. Thank You for new life and a fresh start. You make all things new. Help me remember that Your mercies are new every morning and great is Your faithfulness. May I remember that I am born again and a child of God.*

R 28

"I'm sorry!"

We moms often have to apologize when we yell at our kids, "recycle" a school art project, or forget about a promised special outing. And we teach our children to say "I'm sorry" nearly every day when they do something wrong. This teaches them how relationships are made right. After apologizing, we all experience the good feeling of "making up."

> "For you have been born again, not of perishable seed, but of imperishable, through the living and enduring word of God."
> (1 Peter 1:23)

I'm even more grateful I can regularly go to God and ask for His unlimited forgiveness. Then guilt and condemnation are replaced by freedom and joy. Aren't you thankful you can go straight to God for forgiveness?

But what if you still don't feel good? What if your own heart continues to condemn? What do you do when you just don't *feel* forgiven? What if you desperately need to feel a change of heart?

> *Then Jesus said to her, "Your sins are forgiven." (Luke 7:48)*

A Changed Heart... Is Forgiven—Carrie

Day Two

Carrie met Samuel in college when they studied together in his dorm room. Carrie and Sam's study sessions escalated into much more, and when Carrie became pregnant they chose to terminate the pregnancy. Shortly thereafter, they were engaged, and a year and a half later, they married and began their journey back to God.

Carrie could hardly believe God still loved her. Though she grieved the loss of their child, confessed the sin, and asked for God's forgiveness, Carrie stumbled between doubt and assurance, fear and faith. And Samuel echoed her feelings of pain when he wrote, "Every time I see a child I want to scream; it's all I can do to keep from crying. . . ." Carrie could not shake the paralyzing terror and deep despair. She needed counseling but didn't want to admit depression or anxiety disorder.

> "So if the Son sets you free, you will be free indeed." (John 8:36)

Ultimately, Carrie knew God had forgiven them, but she couldn't forgive herself.

In time, she began to understand God's forgiveness, goodness, and grace. Five years later they both felt ready to have children. Samuel had earned his doctorate and Carrie had begun teaching. Still another eight years went by, and they remained childless—longing for a child, missing someone they'd never even met. Carrie couldn't help but think her infertility was punishment for destroying the life God had given her. Why would He entrust her with another? Though their home felt empty, the two were each other's best friends. They picnicked in the park, walked in the woods, or rowed a boat on the lake.

When they began infertility testing, the blood work brought bad news: Carrie would need aggressive hormone therapy because she was approaching early menopause.

The first step in the process involved x-rays. As Carrie sat on a metal table dressed only in a hospital gown, her heart raced, and her hands sweated. "I don't want to be here. I don't want to do this. No!" She recognized this position, those same words, the same fears, and the same feelings from so many years before. Although the procedure triggered an irrational, illogical response based on her past, it also offered them hope for a new life.

"No! I can't do this," she said. And in so doing, Carrie gave up any medical intervention to improve her chance of pregnancy. Her husband's understanding led them to return to their original desire to adopt.

Sooner than they were ready, they found they were first on the list and the mother-to-be was due in three weeks! Then Carrie, like so many other mothers-to-be, doubted whether she would be a good mom. "Maybe my students are my kids. There's lots of ways to be around children without being a mom. Should I just pour my efforts into that? Do we even deserve to be parents? Would we be good parents? Lord, what is your will for us?" Then she "just happened" to read "He settles the barren woman in her home as a happy mother of children. Praise the LORD" (Psalms 113:9). Could it be any clearer?

The birth mother had two desires. She wanted Carrie present at the birth and for baby AJ (Aaron Joshua) to come home directly from the hospital with Sam and Carrie. Carrie was so grateful for both privileges. She knew she'd be able to tell her son about his birthday. What kid doesn't love to hear that story over and over again?

Now Carrie tells her son what a head of hair he had, and how in mere seconds, through expert nurse swaddling, he became a football with a knit-capped head. And then, of course, she remembers the moment when after so many years of imagining and hoping and moving through heartache to healing, they placed AJ in her arms.

As Aaron grew, they learned of his developmental delays and wondered if he would ever speak. Still, they were determined to love him just like God created him and to patiently help him overcome his weaknesses. Now five years later, they can barely get him to stop singing and asking questions!

> "I write to you, dear children, because your sins have been forgiven on account of his name."
> (1 John 2:12)

What would Carrie say she wished she understood? The head-to-heart knowledge about compassion and forgiveness. She knew God forgave her, but she had a hard time living out that belief. "How important it is to live firmly believing in the totality of forgiveness! To unload that doubting baggage so an even greater joy could be experienced!"

Luke 7:37–47 has become dear to Carrie.

When a woman who had lived a sinful life in that town learned that Jesus was eating at the Pharisee's house, she brought an alabaster jar of perfume, and as she stood behind him at his feet weeping, she began to wet his feet with her tears. Then she wiped them with her hair, kissed them and poured perfume on them.

When the Pharisee who had invited him saw this, he said to himself, "If this man were a prophet, he would know who is touching him and what kind of woman she is—that she is a sinner." Jesus answered him, "Simon, I have something to tell you."

"Tell me, teacher," he said.

"Two men owed money to a certain moneylender. One owed him five hundred denarii, and the other fifty. Neither of them had the money to pay him back, so he canceled the debts of both. Now which of them will love him more?"

Simon replied,

"I suppose the one who had the bigger debt canceled."

"You have judged correctly," Jesus said. Then he turned toward the woman and said to Simon, "Do you see this woman? I came into your house. You did not give me any water for my feet, but she wet my feet with her tears and wiped them with her hair. You did not give me a kiss, but this woman, from the time I entered, has not stopped kissing my feet. You did not put oil on my head, but she has poured perfume on my feet. Therefore, I tell you, her many sins have been forgiven—for she loved much. But he who has been forgiven little loves little."

When Carrie read the Luke 7:37–47 passage, she related to the forgiven woman. "What Jesus has done in my life brings me to tears. Now I only hope I imitate her actions, to serve Him without restraint and without care for what others might think and to express my gratitude for His immeasurable love."

1. What do you need to unload? Can you ask for God's forgiveness and then let it all go? David prayed the following prayer after he sinned against God.

Psalms 51:1–12

Have mercy on me, O God, according to your unfailing love; according to your great compassion blot out my transgressions. Wash away all my iniquity and cleanse me from my sin. For I know my transgressions, and my sin is always before me. Against you, you only, have I sinned and done what is evil in your sight, so that you are proved right when you speak and justified when you judge. Surely I was sinful at birth, sinful from the time my mother conceived me. Surely you desire truth in the inner parts; you teach me wisdom in the inmost place. Cleanse me with hyssop, and I will be clean; wash me, and I will be whiter than snow. Let me hear joy and gladness; let the bones you have crushed rejoice. Hide your face from my sins and blot out all my iniquity. Create in me a pure heart, O God, and renew a steadfast spirit within me. Do not cast me from your presence or take your Holy Spirit from me. Restore to me the joy of your salvation and grant me a willing spirit, to sustain me.

> "Let us draw near to God with a sincere heart in full assurance of faith, having our hearts sprinkled to cleanse us from a guilty conscience and having our bodies washed with pure water." (Hebrews 10:22)

_____

_____

_____

2. How could asking for God's forgiveness help you become a better wife and Mom?

_____

_____

_____

My friend Marci writes, "Forgive yourself, no matter what you do or don't do, He's already forgiven the mess. Don't re-create it; instead, get down to business, clean up, and go forward. You will feel better and so will your family."

Have you ever considered you have *much love* because you have been *much forgiven*?

3. Micah 7:19 says, "You will again have compassion on us; you will tread our sins underfoot and hurl all our iniquities into the depths of the sea." And Psalms 103:12 says, *"As far as the east is from the west, so far has he removed our transgressions from us."* If you're struggling with the ability to *feel* His forgiveness, can you list persons you might be able to talk to for help?

_____

_____

_____

4. Read the following psalm aloud as praise to the Lord.

> "Blessed are they whose transgressions are forgiven, whose sins are covered. Blessed is the man whose sin the Lord will never count against him." (Romans 4:7–8)

Psalm 103 (emphasis added)

*Praise the L*ORD*, O my soul; all my inmost being, praise his holy name.*

*Praise the L*ORD*, O my soul, and forget not all his benefits—*

*who **forgives** all your sins and heals all your diseases,*

*who **redeems** your life from the pit and crowns you with love and compassion,*

*who **satisfies** your desires with good things so that your youth is renewed like the eagle's.*

*The L*ORD *works righteousness and justice for all the oppressed.*

He made known his ways to Moses, his deeds to the people of Israel:

*The L*ORD *is **compassionate** and **gracious**, **slow to anger**, **abounding in love**.*

He will not always accuse, nor will he harbor his anger forever; he does not treat us as our sins deserve or repay us according to our iniquities.

*For as high as the heavens are above the earth, **so great is his love** for those who fear him; as far as the east is from the west, **so far has he removed our transgressions** from us.*

***As a father has compassion** on his children, so the*

LORD has compassion on those who fear him; for he knows how we are formed, he remembers that we are dust.

As for man, his days are like grass, he flourishes like a flower of the field;

the wind blows over it and it is gone, and its place remembers it no more.

But from everlasting to everlasting **the LORD's love is with those who fear him**, and his righteousness with their children's children—with those who keep his covenant and remember to obey his precepts.

The LORD has established his throne in heaven, and his kingdom rules over all.

Praise the LORD, you his angels, you mighty ones who do his bidding, who obey his word.

Praise the LORD, all his heavenly hosts, you his servants who do his will.

Praise the LORD, all his works everywhere in his dominion. Praise the LORD, O my soul.

5. According to the opening of this psalm, what three things does the Lord do?

_____

_____

_____

6. How high is His love and what does that mean to you?

_____

_____

_____

7. How far has He removed our transgressions? (The points of the compass: north, south, east, and west form a cross).

_____

_____

_____

8. Underline words that describe God.

9. Memorize another verse to add to your collection. To help memorize, sometimes I break a passage into sections and memorize the hardest part first.

In him we have redemption through his blood, the forgiveness of sins, in accordance with the riches of God's grace. (Ephesians 1:7)

Response:

10. If you're struggling with forgiveness, pray this portion of Psalm 103 in closing.

I have asked Your forgiveness but have not always felt it. I claim Your love, grace, and forgiveness.

You forgive all my sins and heal all my diseases; you redeemed my life from the pit and crowned me with love and compassion. You are compassionate and gracious, slow to anger, abounding in love.

You will not always accuse, nor harbor anger forever. You do not treat me as my sins deserve or repay me according to my iniquities. For as high as the heavens are above the earth, so great is Your love for those who fear You; as far as the east is from the west, so far have You removed my transgressions from me. As a father has compassion on his children, so You have compassion on those who fear You; Your love is from everlasting to everlasting to those who fear You.

Friend, if you prayed this prayer to the Lord, He has heard you and has forgiven you!

Perhaps Carrie's story reminded you of God's forgiveness. When you say, "I'm sorry," with a repentant heart, God says, "I forgive you." With His forgiveness as your model, you are commanded to forgive others. Not only will you teach your children to say, "I'm sorry," you will teach and model, "I forgive you," and demonstrate the freedom and joy offered to *a heart that forgives.*

Be kind and compassionate to one another, forgiving each other, just as in Christ God forgave you. (Ephesians 4:32)

At best, Sandra's mom and dad were absentee parents. Sandra's mother was bipolar and in and out of mental institutions; her father was a functional alcoholic who drank himself to sleep each night. Sandra had no models for her parenting.

Though Mom and Dad were physically present, they were emotionally removed and unloving. Sandra cannot remember any individual attention, meaningful conversation, or ever hearing the words, "I'm sorry." She found it impossible to please her parents. When she was punished, it was severe, bordering on abusive, and mixed with unkind words. Unfortunately, her parents were repeating a system of punishment meted out on them as children, and the "sins of the father" (Exodus 20:5) continued.

Sandra did not want to continue the cycle. She knew she had to start over.

But to do so, she needed to let go of the past. When asked, "If you were five steps ahead and could advise someone walking behind you, what would you tell them about how to pack for the journey of motherhood?" Sandra answered that moms first need to unpack!

> "But one thing I do: Forgetting what is behind and straining toward what is ahead, I press on toward the goal to win the prize for which God has called me heavenward in Christ Jesus." (Philippians 3:13–14)

Women need to work through their issues with a counselor, a minister, and through prayer. You have to evaluate lingering anger, resentment, hurt feelings, and childhood issues, and put them behind you. If you have something important you want to do prior to kids, get it out of the way first because you'll need to focus on your children once you have them. A mother too focused on her ambitions or problems will have a difficult time giving time and love to her children. —*Sandra*

Sandra spoke from experience; she had learned the hard way.

Second, Sandra realized she had a choice: she could become bitter or better. She chose the latter, but not without much thought and prayer. She pleaded with God to keep her from bitter feelings toward her parents and struggled with how to honor them as they continued to disappoint her. "My parents may catch me off guard every now and again, or an old 'issue' that I thought I had dealt with may rear its ugly head from time to time, or I may feel a pang of envy when I see a friend's doting parents/grandparents. I just pray about it as I go along; it's a work in progress." Sandra continues to pray for her parents and honor them.

> For if you forgive men when they sin against you, your heavenly Father will also forgive you. But if you do not forgive men their sins, your Father will not forgive your sins.
> (Matthew 6:14–15)

Third, Sandra needed a vision for motherhood. She asked help from godly women and from God Himself. Through the years, she asked God to shape her family and has relied on her relationship with Him. He has equipped her to accomplish His purposes. She relates, "I can only do so much; if I cover my children in prayer, then I can have peace that God is in charge."

Though her past didn't seem to prepare her for the future, she began to realize even handicaps could be used for good. She claimed Romans 8:28, "And we know that in all things God works for the good of those who love him, who have been called according to his purpose." Sandra is now the busy mother of four boys. Though she did not—and seemingly cannot—have the loving relationship she had longed for with her parents, she is creating it for her children. "If I didn't learn how to love from my parents, at least I learned how *not* to love."

She looks at the positive:

> I don't have enough time in a day to focus on the negative. God will never give me more challenges than I can handle. He knows my needs and will give me the strength. With God's help, I believe I can break this chain; I want my children to grow up feeling like they are special just as God made them, and I want them to feel loved unconditionally.

With the idea of unpacking, look at these scriptures and determine what to unload and what to pack.

1. From the verses below, circle what you should do (verses 1–2), and cross out everything you should unpack.

_____

_____

_____

Colossians 3:1–10

Since, then, you have been raised with Christ, set your hearts on things above, where Christ is seated at the right hand of God. Set your minds on things above, not on earthly things. For you died, and your life is now hidden with Christ in God. When Christ, who is your life, appears, then you also will appear with him in glory.

Put to death, therefore, whatever belongs to your earthly nature: sexual immorality, impurity, lust, evil desires and greed, which is idolatry. Because of these, the wrath of God is coming. You used to walk in these ways, in the life you once lived. But now you must rid yourselves of all such things as these: anger, rage, malice, slander, and filthy language from your lips. Do not lie to each other, since you have taken off your old self with its practices and have put on the new self, which is being renewed in knowledge in the image of its Creator.

Our new self is being renewed in the image of our Creator! What a wonderful thought! No matter what your past, you are new in Christ. He can help you in your parenting and give you a fresh start. Ephesians 4:22–24 confirms that "You were taught, with regard to your former way of life, to put off your old self, which is being corrupted by its deceitful desires; to be made new in the attitude of your minds; and to put on the new self, created to be like God in true righteousness and holiness."

2. Look at the following verses, and write a list of what to *put off* and what to *put on*.

Ephesians 4:31–32

Get rid of all bitterness, rage and anger, brawling and slander, along with every form of malice. Be kind and compassionate to one another, forgiving each other, just as in Christ God forgave you.

Colossians 3:12–14

Therefore, as God's chosen people, holy and dearly loved, clothe yourselves with compassion, kindness, humility, gentleness and patience. Bear with each other and forgive whatever grievances you may have against one another. Forgive as the Lord forgave you. And over all these virtues put on love, which binds them all together in perfect unity.

Put Off:	Put On:

As you dress and undress each day, the action of *putting off* and *putting on* clothes can be a physical reminder to put on the right attitude of compassion, kindness, humility, gentleness, patience, forgiveness, and love.

Sandra decided to *put off* bitterness and anger, and to *put on* compassion and love. Sandra chose to forgive her parents and in so doing, became a more loving parent. If she had held on to anger and refused to forgive, it would only have harmed her and others around her. Unforgiveness has a rippling effect. An angry spirit and unforgiving heart invites darkness.

3. What things do you need to put off or on? Be specific. For example, "I need to show more kindness to my husband."

To put something on or off is not accidental, it's a choice you make every day.

_____

_____

_____

4. What one new idea can you think about and take away from the following three verses?

_____

_____

_____

But whoever hates his brother is in the darkness and walks around in the darkness; he does not know where he is going, because the darkness has blinded him. (1 John 2:11)

If you forgive anyone, I [Paul] also forgive him. And what I have forgiven—if there was anything to forgive—I have forgiven in the sight of Christ for your sake, in order that Satan might not outwit us. For we are not unaware of his schemes. (2 Corinthians 2:10–11)

"In your anger do not sin": Do not let the sun go down while you are still angry, and do not give the devil a foothold. (Ephesians 4:26–27)

Something to think about

_____   _____

📖 5. In closing, read Hebrews 12:1–2 below (emphasis added) and note the underlined words.

_____

_____

_____

> "And when you stand praying, if you hold anything against anyone, forgive him, so that your Father in heaven may forgive you your sins."
> (Mark 11:25)

*Therefore, since we are surrounded by such a great cloud of witnesses, **let us throw off** everything that **hinders** and the sin that so easily **entangles,** and **let us run*** *with perseverance* the race marked out for us. **Let us fix our eyes on Jesus,** *the author and perfecter of our faith, who for the joy set before him endured the cross, scorning its shame, and sat down at the right hand of the throne of God.*

> "Do not repay evil with evil or insult with insult, but with blessing, because to this you were called so that you may inherit a blessing." (1 Peter 3:9)

6. "Let us throw off . . ." If there is anything that hinders or entangles your faith, your marriage, or your parenting, it's time to throw it off. Is there anything you might need to pray about or bring to a Christian friend or counselor?

_____

_____

_____

"Let us fix our eyes on Jesus." Since Jesus forgave you, and because He is the author and perfecter of your faith, you need to forgive others. Practicing this prepares you for motherhood. You will need to forgive your children and even more importantly, ask them to forgive you.

You can do it! It's possible through His grace, strength, and love. And along with those new clothes . . . how about a new heart as well?

> *I will give you a new heart and put a new spirit in you; I will remove from you your heart of stone and give you a heart of flesh. And I will put my Spirit in you and move you to follow my decrees and be careful to keep my laws. (Ezekiel 36:26–27)*

Response: *Lord, help me fix my eyes on You as you perfect my faith. You endured so much more than I ever have or will. Let me throw off everything that hinders me and run the race with perseverance. Help me find good counsel. Daily reveal in me anything that may cause me to stumble in my parenting. Give me a new and tender heart, and a spirit of forgiveness.*

When I asked my friend Jen what she wished she had known before she became a parent, she radiated a smile and said, "Not to try to force a square peg in a round hole." Then she went on to say what so many other moms had. "Why do we compare our kids with others and expect them to be something they are not?" A life-threatening emergency, taught Jen to consider her heart's desires.

A Changed Heart...
Is a Heart of No Compare—Jen

> *I praise you because I am fearfully and wonderfully made; your works are wonderful, I know that full well. (Psalms 139:14)*

When Jen had her first child, she felt almost annoyed that Kelly wouldn't behave like her friend's daughter. "Why can't my daughter just stand by my side at the store instead of flitting around like a butterfly?" Kelly was dramatic and energetic and never followed directions without resistance. "At her first ballet recital, I cringed as my daughter broke off and did her own routine during the performance."

Then she worried about her second born. Conor was domineering, critical of others, and sometimes a bully. When things didn't go his way, he became grumpy and complained excessively. "I was frustrated that other boys could let things roll off their backs, but he became distressed for a long time. What was I doing wrong?" When Conor entered first grade, Jen learned to appreciate Conor's differences. "Conor's loving first-grade teacher always had a way of turning what I saw as weaknesses into strengths. Bossiness became leadership; complaining became seeking justice."

Similarly, Jen noted that what appeared to be stubbornness and disobedience in Kelly when Jen thought a project was "good enough" was actually Kelly's quest for perfection. Kelly had a God-given eye for detail and a love for making and giving gifts. Discovering Kelly's love language, natural talents, and heart's desire helped Jen understand her daughter. Jen realized, "If only I could have looked at my children with eyes like the Father looks at me!"

A year later, Jen and her husband Drew were expecting their third child. Everything about this pregnancy and baby was unique. Though Jen wasn't due until November, in August, Jen's body went into shock and both mother and child were in danger. Jen's pre-eclampsia meant the doctors had to take the baby immediately.

Their daughter was born two months early, at one-pound, thirteen ounces, and because of pressure on the brain, a drainage tube was inserted into her head just below the skin to allow fluid to flow from her brain into her abdomen. When the baby stabilized, the doctors thought she might go home on Halloween. That really scared Jen. Was her daughter ready to come home? But then the baby contracted bacterial meningitis, and the doctors explained that her little four-pound body might not be able to fight off the infection. They were told to call their pastor and get ready to say, "good bye." But God had other plans.

Kelly and Conor named their baby sister. Kelly chose Gabrielle and Conor chose Joy, and so Gabrielle Joy became Gigi—God's Little Girl. All through Gigi's lengthy hospitalization and her battle for life, she remained God's little girl. On Christmas Eve, Jen and Drew surprised Kelly and Connor by covering Gigi's car seat with a hole-punched gift-wrapped box and placing it on the front porch. They rang the doorbell and ran, and when the kids answered and lifted the present, Conor and Kelly squealed, "Gigi's home!"

Gigi still struggles, and obstacles remain, but still Jen celebrates Gigi's uniqueness.

> The ironic thing is that with Kelly and Conor, I was so concerned with molding them into perfect little beings that I didn't really enjoy them (in all their uniqueness) to the fullest! And now I have little Gigi, who is very "imperfect" by the world's standards. But I celebrate and revel in her smallest accomplishments. I truly am experiencing joy with her, with the uniqueness with which God created her. I wish I had truly appreciated and celebrated the specific qualities in Kelly and Conor at a young age, instead of trying to make them more like me! I love who they have become and the character traits that now shine in them. —*Jen*

The evening Jen related her story, I looked around our table at the food court and delighted in the children. Though ten-year-old Kelly had a friend with her and didn't really know my daughter Christine, Kelly asked her questions worthy of adult conversation, "So, Christine, what sort of things do you like to do after school?" Through Kelly's persistent friendliness, the three became fast friends at one end of the table while the baby smiled, and Conor, outnumbered by girls six-to-one, sat politely without complaining at the other end of the table. We fellowshipped over French fries as Jen radiated a joy and confidence in her children and in the God who created her children special and unique.

Heartwork

1. Imagine your children a few years from now. Considering the topics below, list all the things you've always dreamed or hoped for them.

PERSONALITY:

_____
_____
_____

APPEARANCE:

_____
_____
_____

TALENTS:

_____
_____
_____

HEALTH:

_____
_____
_____

SPIRITUAL GROWTH:

_____
_____
_____

MENTAL CAPACITY:

_____

_____

_____

PHYSICAL SKILLS:

_____

_____

_____

2. Are any of these areas really necessary or important? If you could only pick one or two qualities or talents for your child, what would they be?

_____

_____

_____

et your child be a kid—don't try to mold his personality and likes/dislikes too much into someone who's just a complement to you. Be hopeful and excited about waiting to see who God unfolds him to be. —Lori

This exercise helped me learn what I really wanted. I hope my daughters Christine and Julia are kind to others and that their love of the Lord draws others to Him.

3. In Jesus' Sermon on the Mount, He talked about storing up treasures in heaven instead of treasures on earth (Matthew 6:19–21). Of course you love and treasure your children, but what is wrong with treasuring their talents and achievements?

_____

_____

4. Later in Matthew 6, Jesus explains to seek first His kingdom and His righteousness (verse 33). With that in mind, how should we direct our children's gifts and talents?

_____

_____

_____

Eric Liddell, the Olympic athlete whose life was depicted in the film, *Chariots of Fire*, was born to run. He derived great pleasure from his God-given talent, and then ran a greater race to the glory of God. At the height of his career, he left the racing track for China to use another God-given talent: sharing the gospel.

God gives each child special talents that need nurturing. Even before birth, God bestows certain physical, emotional, and mental characteristics on your child.

5. Underline everything in the following passages that emphasizes how early on God is involved in our lives from the beginning.

> *"Before I formed you in the womb I knew you, before you were born I set you apart" (Jeremiah 1:5)*

> *For you created my inmost being; you knit me together in my mother's womb. I praise you because I am fearfully and wonderfully made; your works are wonderful, I know that full well. My frame was not hidden from you when I was made in the secret place. When I was woven together in the depths of the earth (Psalms 139:13–15)*

> *Yet you brought me out of the womb; you made me trust in you even at my mother's breast. From birth I was cast upon you; from my mother's womb you have been my God. (Psalms 22:9–10)*

Even in the womb, a child has a certain personality, mannerisms, and purpose. My friend Holly's son, Jacob, was not a thumb sucker; instead he chose his third and fourth fingers, and even sucked on them for his ultrasound picture!

In the Bible, another Jacob grasped for something even in the womb, then later stole his twin brother's birthright, wrestled with securing a wife, struggled with an angel, and ultimately wrestled with God. "In the womb he grasped his brother's heel; as a man he struggled with God. He struggled with the angel and overcame him; he wept and begged for his favor" (Hosea 12:3–4). Jacob wrestled with his prenatal personality throughout his entire life.

Similarly, the baby John leaped for joy in his mother's womb when he heard Mary's voice and knew Jesus was near (Luke 1:41–44). He became John the Baptist and went on to announce and baptize the Lamb of God (John 1:29)!

These three examples show how uniquely God created children. Your children can know that God knit them together and they are fearfully and wonderfully made. Whether aged three or thirteen, children find encouragement in knowing their uniqueness. My friend Lisa reminds her children of it each night as they go to bed. "I reword parts of Psalms 139 and tell my children every night who they are.

You

were knit together in mommy's womb
Are fearfully and wonderfully made

All the days of your life were ordained by God
You
Are redeemed by Jesus
Are filled with the Holy Spirit
Are loved by Mommy and Daddy
That's who you are."

6. Jacob was different from his brother Esau. Cain was different from Abel, and Absalom from Solomon. Understanding that each child is unique, how do you handle the challenges of differing sibling personalities?

_____

_____

_____

Sometimes parents want or expect too much for or from their children. And maybe it's not just for their children, but for themselves. Matthew 20:20–28 reveals that Jesus understood one mother's rather prideful intent. The mother of Zebedee's sons came to Jesus with her sons, knelt down, and asked Jesus for a favor: "Grant that one of these two sons of mine may sit at your right and the other at your left in your kingdom."

Jesus explained that the decision of who would sit at those places belonged to His father. The disciples were angry, and Jesus reiterated,

Whoever wants to become great among you must be your servant, and whoever wants to be first must be your slave—just as the Son of Man did not come to be served, but to serve, and to give his life as a ransom for many. (Matthew 20:26–28)

7. How can we raise our children to look not for places of honor, but to serve?

_____

_____

_____

The world says, "Climb to the top"; Jesus says, "The first shall be last." The world looks at the appearance, the height, and the strength. But when the Lord directed Samuel to choose the next king, God pointed out the young, small shepherd boy.

But the LORD said to Samuel, "Do not consider his appearance or his height, for I have rejected him. The LORD does not look at the things man looks at. Man looks at the outward appearance, but the LORD looks at the heart." (1 Samuel 16:7)

8. Man looks at the outward appearance, but what does the Lord look at?

_____

When encountered with giant problems, this young shepherd boy with *a heart for God* courageously stood on the name of God and believed he would be delivered (1 Samuel 17).

9. Teaching character qualities to your child is important. Underline qualities in the passage below that you would like to teach your child.

For this very reason, make every effort to add to your faith goodness; and to goodness, knowledge; and to knowledge, self-control; and to self-control, perseverance; and to perseverance, godliness; and to godliness, brotherly kindness; and to brotherly kindness, love. For if you possess these qualities in increasing measure, they will keep you from being ineffective and unproductive in your knowledge of our Lord Jesus Christ. (2 Peter 1:5–8)

How precious that the Lord uniquely created your child with a purpose. What a privilege to parent your child to seek after Him, follow Him, and become *effective* and *productive* in his knowledge of Jesus. To be all God created him to be! In closing, my friend Sherrill reminds us of the special place God has given children.

> God makes each one of us uniquely and knows us even before we enter the world. There's something very touching and special about knowing He knows us. He has made us a little lower than the angels. Infants and children bring glory to Him just by their very being and existing. If we love the Lord and trust Him in our parenting, He will work out all things for good. —*Sherrill*

Response: This closing prayer is from Psalm 8.

> *O LORD, our LORD, how majestic is your name in all the earth! You have set your glory above the heavens. From the lips of children and infants you have ordained praise because of your enemies, to silence the foe and the avenger. When I consider your heavens, the work of your fingers, the moon and the stars, which you have set in place, what is man that you are mindful of him, the son of man that you care for him? You made him a little lower than the heavenly beings and crowned him with glory and honor.*

With the impending birth of her first child, Tina longed to know more about Jesus and His Word. Her first child caused her to let go of the past, have a heart for the Bible, and to depend on God for wisdom.

A Changed Heart... Gets A Fresh Start
in the Word—Tina

Like newborn babies, crave pure spiritual milk, so that by it you may grow up in your salvation. (1 Peter 2:2)

When Tina was six, her father died in a car accident, leaving Tina, her mother, and her three-year-old brother alone. Within a year, her mother married a military man whom Tina did not trust. Forced to call him dad, she and her brother assumed his last name and moved from the only place they called home.

Before long, his authoritarian discipline style expressed itself. Harsh insults formed wounds that would not heal. Tina couldn't do anything right, and so she felt inadequate and unloved. Inwardly she rebelled and determined he would not destroy her. While at Virginia Tech, Tina became a Christian, and a friend gave her a Bible she still uses. Inside the cover her friend wrote, "I love you. I hope you get into the Word."

After Tina married and became pregnant with her first child, she felt completely overwhelmed and incapable. All the deeply buried wounds surfaced. Haunted by all the mistakes she knew she would make, she feared she would hurt her child like she had been hurt. "I knew God was watching over me, and I knew He cared, but I didn't understand I could have a personal relationship with Him. I wish I could have used the Bible as a resource and known all the promises of God."

Though plagued by childhood wounds, Tina learned what it meant to be a child of God and to find her strength in Him.

God blessed her with Alexa and Megan. "My girls made me want to be a better person, and that brought me to the Bible, which I think was His plan."

That didn't mean everything would be simple. She had to filter difficult life experiences through her ever-growing faith. Her husband was a United Airlines pilot who was

> "Yet to all who received him, to those who believed in his name, he gave the right to become children of God—children born not of natural descent, nor of human decision or a husband's will, but born of God."
> (John 1:12–13)

on duty and in flight on September 11, 2001. Later, the DC sniper kept her children from playing on the playground, and as a former student at Virginia Tech, she was personally stung by the senseless tragedy on that campus. Those stressful times led her to "get into the Word" like her college friend hoped.

Becoming a mother helped Tina grow as a child of God. Her desire to develop a hunger in the girls inspires her to teach the Word in fresh and creative ways. Not only does she now "get into the Word," Tina teaches a fifth-grade Sunday school class and has led a bi-weekly Bible study group of third, fourth, and fifth grade girls. Though Tina doesn't always feel adequate for the task, she pours herself into studying right along with the girls.

The miracle in her motherhood is that she discovered she should never have been able to have children. Because Tina's mother was exposed to DES, a synthetic estrogen now banned, Tina was born with multiple deformities including half a uterus, one functioning ovary, one functioning kidney, and a malformed fallopian tube. With all that, it was a miracle she got pregnant. At a recent doctor appointment, two different doctors explained to her they had never heard of a woman exposed to DES being able to bear children. God had other plans.

Heartwork

Tina felt inadequate and spiritually unprepared. Maybe you feel that way, too. I think most moms-to-be want *to be* better persons. I remember being concerned about purity. How could I watch another soap opera? Surely trash television would come out in my life or be a bad example to my children. My friend Lori wrote,

> What habits do you need to begin to change now, before your child—who will imitate your every move and word—arrives? You may not realize just how much of an influence you will have on this little person, and what he will come to believe is acceptable in your house.

Ephesians 5:3–4 warns against the things that are out of place (a hint of sexual immorality, impurity, greed, obscenity, foolish talk, or coarse joking), but encourages thanksgiving.

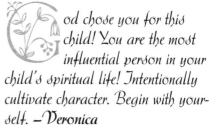

> *Therefore, I urge you, brothers, in view of God's mercy, to offer your bodies as living sacrifices, holy and pleasing to God—this is your spiritual act of worship.*
>
> *Do not conform any longer to the pattern of this world, but be transformed by the renewing of your mind. Then you will be able to test and approve what God's will is—his good, pleasing and perfect will. (Romans 12:1–2)*

God chose you for this child! You are the most influential person in your child's spiritual life! Intentionally cultivate character. Begin with yourself. —Veronica

1. Are there areas in your life that might not be holy or pleasing to the Lord? In what areas do you need to transform and renew your mind?

_____

_____

_____

Tina also wished she had a stronger foundation. If you don't have a background in Christ, where can you begin? Doing a Bible study is a great start. Let's look at a few practices that could make your daily time in God's Word easier.

"I will set before my eyes no vile thing." (Psalms 101:3)

1. First, choose your next Bible study. Would you like to go solo on a published study or join a group of women? Go to a Christian bookstore and find a study that addresses your current needs, or seek out women's studies in local churches. Community Bible Study (CBS) http://www.communitybiblestudy.org/ and Bible Study Fellowship (BSF) http://www.bsfinternational .org/ are great places to begin, and these organizations work to provide childcare. Make a plan, even today, to look into a local group.

_____

_____

_____

Or perhaps you'd like to study the Bible on your own, without filling in any blanks in a book. If so, pick up your Bible and notice how it's built into two sections: the Old and New Testaments. These two sections contain different types of books. If you understand the differences, you'll better understand how to study these books. If you're studying on your own, choose a book—perhaps one of the four gospels (Matthew, Mark, Luke, or John), and read it from beginning to end.

Ask yourself simple questions that begin with Who, What, Where, and When, and then go deeper and think of *"How* does that mean I should live?" or *"Why* would Jesus include that teaching?" Ask O-I-A questions: What does it say? *Observation.* What does it mean? *Interpretation.* What does it mean to me? *Application.*

These resources may help you study on your own:

How to Read the Bible for All It's Worth by Gordon Fee and Douglas Stuart (Grand Rapids, MI: Zondervan, 2003)

How to Read the Bible Book by Book: A Guided Tour by Gordon Fee and Douglas Stuart (Zondervan, 2002).

How to Study the Bible for Yourself by Tim LaHaye (Eugene, OR: Harvest House Publishers, 2006).

Fill in the Blanks: I think I'd like to begin with the Bible study titled _____ _____ or study through the book of _____.

2. Pick up a journal for yourself and jot down your favorite verses. Get in the habit of gathering truths you can pass on to your children. Collect the promises of God. Here are two to begin: "Delight yourself in the LORD and he will give you the desires of your heart. Commit your way to the LORD; trust in him and he will do this" (Psalms 37:4–5).

_____

_____

_____

Don't just collect promises; begin memorizing verses to hold in your heart that will spill out in your life. My former minister used to pray, "Teach me, that others may be taught." You need to be taught so you have something to teach your children. The truths you collect, understand, and memorize, you can pass on to your children. In my early twenties I heard the minister's wife explain how she read Psalm 136 to her children and how they echoed with the words, "His love endures forever." I could hardly wait to try that on my own children. Though I had to wait another decade!

3. Memorize Psalms 119:105: "Your **word** is a lamp to my feet and a light for my path."

_____

_____

_____

Memorizing tools:
Picture the verse as a scene.

Act it out or draw it.

Sing it!

Write the verse over and over.

Write it and read it. Each time you re-read the verse, cross out another word until you have it completely memorized.

Write the verse on a 3 x 5 card and carry it with you to meditate on.

Don't forget to memorize the reference or road marker. This will guide you back to the verse and help direct others to it.

4. Read the excerpts from Psalm 119 below, which talk about how you need to know God's statutes, obey His precepts, and follow them with all your heart. To discover how important God's Words are to God and to the psalmist, underline the following words from the passage: "statutes," "commands," "precepts," "law," "decrees," "ways," and "word."

> "My son, do not forget my teaching, but keep my commands in your heart, for they will prolong your life many years and bring you prosperity."
>
> (Proverbs 3:1–2)

_____

_____

_____

Blessed are they whose ways are blameless, who walk according to the law of the LORD. Blessed are they who keep his statutes and seek him with all their heart. They do nothing wrong; they walk in his ways. You have laid down precepts that are to be fully obeyed. Oh, that my ways were steadfast in obeying your decrees! Then I would not be put to shame when I consider all your commands. I will praise you with an upright heart as I learn your righteous laws. I will obey your decrees; do not utterly forsake me. (verses 1–8)

How can a young man keep his way pure? By living according to your word. I seek you with all my heart; do not let me stray from your commands. I have hidden your word in my heart that I might not sin against you. Praise be to you, o LORD; teach me your decrees. With my lips I recount all the laws that come from your mouth. I rejoice in following your statutes as one rejoices in great riches. I meditate on your precepts and consider your ways. I delight in your decrees; I will not neglect your word. (verses 9–16)

The law from your mouth is more precious to me than thousands of pieces of silver and gold. (verse 72)

How sweet are your words to my taste, sweeter than honey to my mouth! I gain understanding from your precepts; therefore I hate every wrong path. (verses 103–104)

Great peace have they who love your law, and nothing can make them stumble. (verse 165)

Knowing God's Word and *doing* it are two different things. We need to do more than just *hear* or know God's Word—we need to *do* it. In the Sermon on the Mount, Jesus explained that concept with the following word picture.

Therefore everyone who hears these words of mine and puts them into practice is like a wise man who built his house on the rock. The rain came down, the streams rose, and the winds blew and beat against that house; yet it did not fall, because it had its foundation on the rock. But everyone who hears these words of mine and does not put them into practice is like a foolish man who built his house on sand. The rain came down, the streams rose, and the winds blew and beat against that house, and it fell with a great crash. When Jesus had finished saying these things, the crowds were amazed at his teaching, because he taught as one who had authority, and not as their teachers of the law. (Matthew 7:24–29)

5. How can we build our house on the rock—practically, physically, and spiritually? (v. 24)

_____

_____

_____

6. What does it look like when we build our house on the sand? (v. 26)

_____

_____

_____

7. How does the following verse apply to building your spiritual house? *"By wisdom a house is built, and through understanding it is established; through knowledge its rooms are filled with rare and beautiful treasures"* (Psalms 24:3).

_____

_____

_____

> "Do not merely listen to the word, and so deceive yourselves. Do what it says. Anyone who listens to the word but does not do what it says is like a man who looks at his face in a mirror and, after looking at himself, goes away and immediately forgets what he looks like. But the man who looks intently into the perfect law that gives freedom, and continues to do this, not forgetting what he has heard, but doing it—he will be blessed in what he does." (James 1:22–25)

8. Tina continues to build her house on the Rock and encourage her daughters in their relationships with Jesus. How does studying God's Word help you build your house on the Rock?

_____

_____

_____

Close today's lesson in prayer with more verses from Psalm 119.

Lord, Open my eyes that I may see wonderful things in your law. (verse 18)

Your statutes are my delight; they are my counselors. (verse 24)

Let me understand the teaching of your precepts; then I will meditate on your wonders. My soul is weary with sorrow; strengthen me according to your word. Keep me from deceitful ways; be gracious to me through your law. (verses 27–29)

Direct me in the path of your commands, for there I find delight. Turn my heart toward your statutes and not toward selfish gain. Turn my eyes away from worthless things; preserve my life according to your word. (verses 35–37)

I will walk about in freedom, for I have sought out your precepts. (verse 45)

Your statutes are my heritage forever; they are the joy of my heart. (verse 111)

Direct my footsteps according to your word; let no sin rule over me. (verse 133)

Your promises have been thoroughly tested, and your servant loves them. (verse 140)

Your statutes are forever right; give me understanding that I may live. (verse 144)

I rise before dawn and cry for help; I have put my hope in your word. (verse 147)

An Open Heart

My husband frequently uses the term "expectation management" when describing situations where we have unrealistic hopes. Sometimes mothers need some expectation management. We need a heart of hope, but to also align our hopes with God's desire for our lives. Christy, Becky, Kris, Aimee, and Jane's stories reflect the need for us to understand our new roles. As mothers we will need to learn to serve others, trust God, entrust our children to Him, seek help when there are problems, and accept the gifts He offers.

> **An Open Heart . . .**
>
> Serves—Christy
> Trusts God—Becky
> Entrusts—Kris
> Looks to the Light—Aimee
> Unwraps Gifts—Jane

You have another name! With your first child, you *add* the title of mom and sometimes *lose* a career name or alter it to *working mom.* Either way, it's an adjustment. Some mothers-to-be think the adjustment to motherhood will be blissful and beautiful, and that nurturing will be natural and non-stop. Unfortunately, they may be surprised when motherhood falls short of their expectations.

An Open Heart... Serves—Christy

Day One

> *Do nothing out of selfish ambition or vain conceit, but in humility consider others better than yourselves. Each of you should look not only to your own interests, but also to the interests of others. (Philippians 2:3–4)*

First-time mom, Christy, wondered, "What did I get myself into?" Motherhood was nonstop diapers, feedings, little sleep, and the fear she wasn't doing anything right. Christy had been a career woman who had never respected the stay-at-home mom's non-salaried position. "What do stay-at-home moms do?" she had asked. But now her question was, "Who am I?"

What she didn't know at the time was that though what we do as earthly moms can sometimes seem repetitive, it is eternal. Second Corinthians 4:18 says, "So we fix our eyes not on what is seen, but on what is unseen. For what is seen is temporary, but what is unseen is eternal."

Christy not only struggled with the loss of her old career, she longed for the instruction manual for her new career. And did it have a page on what to do when she didn't have the "mommy" feeling? Would it come? This new role meant trusting God in ways she never had before.

The mommy feelings eventually came. She brightened to see her baby smile for the first time. She studied Austin while he slept and monitored how he experimented with different faces through all kinds of emotions. And when a beloved night of sleep finally came? Yikes, she worried he wasn't all right!

Austin was all right, and so was Christy. And with Lexi, her second child, she understood the baby "ups and downs" and realized she would eventually get a full night's sleep again.

But does she still struggle with her identity? Absolutely. She loves motherhood, but some days she feels she hasn't accomplished anything and lacks self-esteem. It seems she has nothing to show for her work. Like all mothers, her days are filled with repetitive tasks. Pick it up; put it away. Wash it; dry it, and put it away. And there are no performance appraisals, raises, or paychecks to validate her efforts. But then she reminds herself, "How do you measure the outstretched arms of a little child?" And no CEO's praise could compare with, "I love you, Mommy!"

As a mom, Christy discovered she loves to teach Sunday

> *What did I accomplish today? I washed three loads of laundry; I changed eight diapers; I made it to the grocery store without having a meltdown, and I put supper on the table. A job provides work that usually has instant gratification; motherhood provides us with work where you may not see results for months/years to come.*
> *—Karen S., mother of three within four years*

school, art, and cooking. She began a new career that involves teaching children, and though she receives a paycheck, it's not about the money anymore. It's about the satisfaction of giving back the gifts God has given her and investing in the lives of children in immeasurable ways.

She has learned to call on God for patience and direction. She asks, "How am I doing as a mom, God? What should I teach them? Where are we headed?" And she likes to consider all the great things that have happened since she's become a mom.

What about your identity? Do you struggle with the title of "Mommy"? How can you not measure yourself by your accomplishments and the check-offs on your to-do lists, but rather by something much less measurable? Are you ready to serve in new and wonderful ways?

> *Fifteen years from now, my husband and children are not going to remember how clean the house was. They will, however, remember how their wife or mommy tended to them when they had needs. The children will have a model of how to meet the needs of their future spouses and children. They will have a glimpse of what Jesus does for them.* —*Katie*

Heartwork

1. If someone asked, "Who are you?" What would you say?

_____

_____

_____

2. How do you measure your progress? Your success?

_____

_____

_____

3. Do you like to have a to-do list to check off your tasks? If so, what types of things are on your list? Does it make you feel good when the list is completed? How do you feel about doing repetitive tasks? What if you get diverted from your list?

_____

_____

_____

4. With children, how would you define a successful day around your home? (You do not have to say your house was

cleaned top to bottom, that you wrote a novel or canned 57 jars of peaches). How can *being* a daughter of God become a greater priority than *doing* a list of things?

_____

_____

_____

Katie, a young mother with two small children, says,

> As I am planning and working through my day, I try to remember I am a wife and then a mom before I am a short-order-cook, maid, vet, driver, gardener, etc. God put me here to be a wife and mommy before anything else, and it is necessary for me to adjust my expectations to put things in proper perspective. That has helped me tremendously to ease into my role as a new mom.

5. How can you focus on relationships instead of roles?

_____

_____

_____

6. As a mom, you may feel humbled in your servant role. How does Ephesians 6:7–8 apply to you? "Serve wholeheartedly, as if you were serving the Lord, not men, because you know that the Lord will reward everyone for whatever good he does, whether he is slave or free."

_____

_____

_____

Philippians 2:1–5 tells us that our "attitude should be the same as that of Christ Jesus." A part of that means to "Do nothing out of selfish ambition or vain conceit, but in humility consider others better than yourselves. Each of you should look not only to your own interests, but also to the interests of others."

You may not be able to schedule a 45-minute bath, daily workout at the gym, or have the cash for a new outfit. My friend Karen, whose story you will read next week, writes, "It's not about you for the next 18 years! Think about Christ washing His disciples feet in the hours before He went to the cross.

Be ready to serve and pour yourself out for your family and fill up on the Word."

Response: Lord, Help me not to measure myself against other moms or measure my kids against other children. Help me not to build my self-image on things I accomplish, but rather on knowing You. Help me teach my kids to know You, too. As I do my tasks—no matter how many times, may I have a cheerful heart and do everything unto You and in Your name. And may these acts of service bless You and my family.

I am the only person on earth that God has called to be the mother of my children. I continually need to resist the pull and lure to spend my energy doing things other people can do (even if I get more recognition, praise, and external reward for that). I want to continually put my best energy and creativity into being the mother to my children and the wife to my husband. —Lisa

Sometimes things don't work out the way you dreamed. Sometimes the plans for your life go awry. What do you do when you lose hope?

"Do not let your hearts be troubled. Trust in God; trust also in me." (John 14:1)—Jesus

An Open Heart... Trusts God—Becky

Becky married at the age of twenty-two, but she and her husband waited eight years to have children. After struggling with depression, Becky went on medication. During her pregnancy she worried about the medicine's effect on her unborn child. Thankfully, her March baby was a healthy baby girl.

When Kelsey turned five, Becky was excited to be pregnant again. But she lost the baby, and, shortly thereafter, her marriage fell apart, as her husband left her and moved hundreds of miles away. After they divorced, he was in a terrible car accident that left him brain damaged and unable to help with child support. Becky's life wasn't at all what she had anticipated.

Becky explains,

When bad things happen, it's hard for us to see the whole picture like God can. I've heard it's like working on a quilt. We can only see the one square we're working on at the time. God sees the whole quilt beautifully finished. It's hard to let go and just trust God during bad times, especially the ones out of our control, but we must. Everything happens for a reason, and He knows what's best for us.

After the divorce, Becky felt sorry for her daughter and backed off on disciplining or setting rules. Without boundaries, Kelsey began to rebel and throw tantrums. During this time, Becky married Ed, who asked, "Who's the parent and who's the child?" Soon Becky began to set loving boundaries in their home.

Becky learned she needed to be consistent with discipline and to teach values and morals. "You can't be your child's friend. You must be the parent. This is hard sometimes for me especially when Kelsey and I are getting along great and we seem like buddies." And with that comes a lot of patience and understanding. "Love your children unconditionally, and be a stable role model for them. Give them security, and let them be who they truly are—not what you want them to be."

Becky questioned God. Why did all of these things have to happen? And each stage of parenting caused her to question her ability as a mom. Through all the questioning, Becky learned to lean on the Lord and cherish these verses handed down from her grandmother: "Trust in the LORD with all your heart and lean not on your own understanding; in all your ways acknowledge him, and he will make your paths straight" (Proverbs 3:5–6).

Heartwork

Becky found there were times she didn't feel like she was a good role model for mothering. From my interviews, I found every mother feels that way at some point. You may have that experience, too: The "bad mommy days." The days you yell too much, wrongfully blame your child, discipline in anger. You didn't handle things the way God would have wanted. Those experiences are normal. But what are you supposed to do? You've learned you need a heart that is forgiven, a heart that forgives, but you also need to know that as a mom you'll ask God's forgiveness every day. You can trust in His forgiveness, His love, and help to do a better job tomorrow.

And ask your children to forgive you, too. If there are deeper issues, seek counsel. But otherwise, move on. Kicking yourself for yesterday won't make you a better mom today or tomorrow. And as your children change from small, sweet, and cuddly into more independent-minded and sometimes distant teenagers, you may find your parenting skills challenged anew.

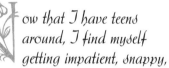 1. Read the following passages from Romans 5:6–11 for encouragement. Underline the words that encourage you.

> You see, at just the right time, when we were still powerless, Christ died for the ungodly. Very rarely will anyone die for a righteous man, though for a good man someone might possibly dare to die. But God demonstrates his own love for us in this: While we were still sinners, Christ died for us.
>
> Since we have now been justified by his blood, how much more shall we be saved from God's wrath through him! For if, when we were God's enemies, we were reconciled to him through the death of his Son, how much more, having been reconciled, shall we be saved through his life! Not only is this so, but we also rejoice in God through our Lord Jesus Christ, through whom we have now received reconciliation.

Now that I have teens around, I find myself getting impatient, snappy, and irritated almost every day. Many days I have been almost in despair at my own childish behavior, and yet God graciously encourages me (when I really deserve chastisement), and I am reminded over and over of Romans 2:4—it's God's kindness that leads us to repentance. He's been showing me a lot of kindness. —Joan

2. How does it make you feel to know that while you were powerless and a sinner, Christ died for you?

_____

_____

_____

On a "good mommy" day, God does not love you more than on a day you yelled at your kids and hid in a closet. God loved you WHEN you were powerless, and WHILE you were sinners, He died for you. This isn't an excuse to sin, but it offers reassurance.

And through the struggles, you will grow. Becky has a strong marriage and a kind, gentle, obedient teenager. Through it all, they've grown in the struggles, which can happen according to Romans 5:1–5.

> "Or do you show contempt for the riches of his kindness, tolerance and patience, not realizing that God's kindness leads you toward repentance?"
>
> (Romans 2:4)

Therefore, since we have been justified through faith, we have peace with God through our Lord Jesus Christ, through whom we have gained access by faith into this grace in which we now stand. And we rejoice in the hope of the glory of God. Not only so, but we also rejoice in our sufferings, because we know that suffering produces perseverance; perseverance, character; and character, hope. And hope does not disappoint us, because God has poured out his love into our hearts by the Holy Spirit, whom he has given us.

3. Write in the progression of our struggles according to this passage:

Sufferings ➔ _____ ➔ _____ ➔ _____

Did you realize sufferings could produce hope? How can you share this with your children? According to Romans 5:5, "Hope does not disappoint us, because God has poured out his love into our hearts by the Holy Spirit, whom he has given us."

_____

_____

_____

4. What can you learn about trust from the following verses? Add your new insights to your trust tank.

Trust Verses	Trust Tank
Those who know your name will trust in you, for you, LORD, have never forsaken those who seek you. (Psalms 9:10) *But blessed is the man who trusts in the LORD, whose confidence is in him.* (Jeremiah 17:7) *But blessed is the man who trusts in the LORD, whose confidence is in him. He will be like a tree planted by the water that sends out its roots by the stream. It does not fear when heat comes; its leaves are always green. It has no worries in a year of drought and never fails to bear fruit.* (Jeremiah 17:7–8) *You will keep in perfect peace him whose mind is steadfast, because he trusts in you.* (Isaiah 26:3) *Trust in the LORD forever, for the LORD, the LORD, is the Rock eternal.* (Isaiah 26:4) *This is a trustworthy saying that deserves full acceptance (and for this we labor and strive), that we have put our hope in the living God, who is the Savior of all men, and especially of those who believe.* (1 Timothy 4:9–10) *Do not let your hearts be troubled. Trust in God; trust also in me.* (John 14:1)	

When unexpected or disappointing events happen, can you also point your children to Jesus and help them learn to trust? These verses are treasures for your children, too. They need to see you rely on Jesus, and they need to practice doing the same.

My friend Lisa reminds me,

> The best thing you can give your child is Jesus. Equip your children to rely on God most of all. Tell them repeatedly, "God is always with you. Call on Him whenever you need Him." It can be such an ego trip to be the center of their world; don't fall for it. Figure out how to point them to Jesus at the same time you are pouring HIS love for them from your heart to theirs.

Trust God no matter what. Remember, " 'Though the mountains be shaken and the hills be removed, yet my unfailing love for you will not be shaken nor my covenant of peace be removed,' says the LORD, who has compassion on you" (Isaiah 54:10).

Response: *Lord, even when life does not go exactly as planned, and I feel like a failure, I know You love me. Help me to remember You are still in control and have a plan for my life. May I grow through the sufferings into a persevering person with character and hope. Help me to model this trust, so my children learn to trust in You, and know that my Hope is in You.*

When I found out I was having twins (with a soon-to-be two-year-old at home), I felt both scared and happy. We did not have a lot of outside help, but together my husband and I made it through all the bottles, diapers, and challenges that come with three kids under the age of three. God believes in you. You are more capable than you realize. Put your trust in Him.
—Brandy

Not only do we need to trust God, we need to entrust our children to Him. My friend Kris, our prayer-group coordinator and a mother of two, served as a short-term missionary to Zambia. Through this experience and what followed, she learned about the need to entrust her children to God.

Do not be anxious about anything, but in everything, by prayer and petition, with thanksgiving, present your requests to God. And the peace of God, which transcends all understanding, will guard your hearts and your minds in Christ Jesus. (Philippians 4:6–7)

Before traveling to Zambia, Kris worried about leaving her children.

> My tendency is to worry, particularly for my children's well being. I had to release them to God and know my life and my children are under His control. I had no contact with my children for two weeks and didn't think I could handle that. When I released them to Him, the peace of God, which transcends all understanding, ruled in my life and my heart. —*Kris*

From her experiences, she advises others to, "Trust in the Lord, and know that your children are His children. He will always love them more, and He will always know far better what is in their best interest than you ever could. Learn to let go, and know that God is in control."

That became a far greater challenge a year later when her first grader was struck with Henoch-Schonlein Purpura, a potentially fatal illness that can permanently damage the kidneys. During the long battle with her son's joint pain, kidney and digestive problems, fevers, and rashes, Kris developed a new and deeper level of trust in God.

> I think the biggest lesson was learning to let go and not to put my child in such a high place that I felt life could not go on if something terrible happened. The night he stopped walking, I wondered if he'd walk again. We went to the ER and prayed, and he walked the next morning. Then he stopped walking again and could not even climb stairs on his belly. When his kidneys started failing and his blood pressure started going up, he just seemed to become sicker than I ever imagined he could be. I started to wonder if he would survive. —*Kris*

For Kris, it was no longer just about asking, "Will he walk again?" and "Will his kidneys function?" It was a question of whether he would live. And whether she could live without him.

That night when I was alone, I started praying and really gave it all to God. I told him I loved my son and was so thankful for the gift He'd given me, and that I really did not want to lose him right now. I let Him know I trusted Him with the outcome whatever it was. I told God out of love for my child, I was asking for him to be healed, but that I trusted God would make the best decision for us. —*Kris*

Kris then slept for five hours, and Ryan began improving the next day. Unfortunately, his health remains somewhat uncertain.

The roller coaster has continued, and Ryan's health has been up and down several times. But each time I try to hand him right back to God through prayer. It is very hard to let go, because I love my child so much. At the same time, God loves him more, and that has really comforted me. —*Kris*

Ryan may recover fully, or he may have another episode, but God is in control.

Heartwork

Motherhood opens us to new emotional experiences. The depth of love and worry are huge. The responsibility of taking care of a young life is pressed upon you, and you suddenly wonder what you would ever do if your child were taken from you.

1. Some moms also experience a new awareness of God's great love for them when they understand how nearly impossible it would be to give up a child. How do the following verses take on new meaning in the context of your

motherhood?

The Word became flesh and made his dwelling among us. We have seen his glory, the glory of the One and Only, who came from the Father, full of grace and truth. (John 1:14)

For God so loved the world that he gave his one and only Son, that whoever believes in him shall not perish but have eternal life. (John 3:16)

This is love: not that we loved God, but that he loved us and sent his Son as an atoning sacrifice for our sins. (1 John 4:10)

But God demonstrates his own love for us in this: While we were still sinners, Christ died for us. (Romans 5:8)

> "For you have been my hope, O Sovereign LORD, my confidence since my youth. From birth I have relied on you; you brought me forth from my mother's womb. I will ever praise you." (Psalms 51:5–6)

_____

_____

_____

2. To begin understanding what God thought of His Son, consider the following passages:

As soon as Jesus was baptized, he went up out of the water. At that moment heaven was opened, and he saw the Spirit of God descending like a dove and lighting on him. And a voice from heaven said, "This is my Son, whom I love; with him I am well pleased." (Mark 3:16–17)

When all the people were being baptized, Jesus was baptized too. And as he was praying, heaven was opened and the Holy Spirit descended on him in bodily form like a dove. And a voice came from heaven: "You are my Son, whom I love; with you I am well pleased." (Mark 3:21–22)

God wants a relationship with you. He loves you so much, He gave up His child so you could be reconciled to Him.

But because of his great love for us, God, who is rich in mercy, made us alive with Christ even when we were dead in transgressions—it is by grace you have been saved. (Ephesians 2:4–5)

But he was pierced for our transgressions,
he was crushed for our iniquities;
the punishment that brought us peace was upon him,
and by his wounds we are healed. (Isaiah 53:5)

Realizing the depth of their love for their own children, some moms expressed sheer amazement that God could love them enough to give up His only Son. But with that knowledge, many moms realized He would also care for their children and that He loved these kids even more than they could.

Tina wrote,

Isaiah 53:5 [above] really spoke to me about my iniquities as a mother. It was like the time I watched *The Passion of the Christ* for the first time. As I watched it, I just felt so overwhelmingly loved . . . and immensely grateful for what He had done for us . . . for me.

God loves you and your children and knows your needs. He knows every intimate detail about you down to the number of hairs on your head. Jesus explains in Luke 12:6–7,

Are not five sparrows sold for two pennies? Yet not one of them is forgotten by God. Indeed, the very hairs of your head are all numbered. Don't be afraid; you are worth more than many sparrows.

Response: Realizing your child is a gift from God, write a prayer dedicating your child to Him. If it helps, incorporate some of the scriptures below.

Trust in the LORD with all your heart and lean not on your own understanding; in all

> "I prayed for this child, and the LORD has granted me what I asked of him. So now I give him to the LORD. For his whole life he will be given over to the LORD." (1 Samuel 1:27–28)

Kris prayed for her child's healing and gave it up to God. Some parents dedicate their children in a church service, thank God for them, commit to raise them in a Christian home, and, like the Old Testament mother Hannah, dedicate their children back to Him.

your ways acknowledge him, and he will make your paths straight. (Proverbs 3:5–6)

Yours, O LORD, is the greatness and the power and the glory and the majesty and the splendor, for everything in heaven and earth is yours. Yours, O LORD, is the kingdom; you are exalted as head over all. Wealth and honor come from you; you are the ruler of all things. In your hands are strength and power to exalt and give strength to all. (1 Chronicles 29:11–12)

Before I formed you in the womb I knew you, before you were born I set you apart (Jeremiah 1:5)

I praise you because I am fearfully and wonderfully made; your works are wonderful, I know that full well. My frame was not hidden from you when I was made in the secret place. When I was woven together in the depths of the earth, your eyes saw my unformed body. All the days ordained for me were written in your book before one of them came to be. (Psalms 139:14–16)

Dear Heavenly Father,

_____

_____

_____

_____

_____

Dedicate your child to God, promising to raise your baby with His guidance, to celebrate Him, and to honor, love, and obey Him. –Kim

Mothers need to know that any children God gives them are not their own, but His, and that He's graciously entrusted them to their care. –Liz

Pick a verse for your child, and make it his/her life verse. Write it on the walls of his/her heart. My daughter Sarah's is, "For he will command his angels concerning you to guard you in all your ways. (Psalms 91:11) –Kim

Some mothers find the joy of motherhood isn't always a joy. And for some it actually brings on darkness and a lack of hope. If you experience the loneliness of depression, or the desperation of anxiety, where do you go for light?

> Send forth your **light** and your truth, let them guide me; let them bring me to your holy mountain, to the place where you dwell. (Psalms 43:3)

An Open Heart... Seeks the Light—Aimee

Aimee never considered that marriage or motherhood would be difficult. Aimee married a man in Christian ministry, but their first year of marriage was disastrous and they both thought they had made a terrible mistake. After pulling in separate directions, they took a time-out from ministry. Her husband pursued another career, and through counseling and time, their marriage healed. As they grew closer to God and one another, they both concluded he should return to the ministry.

Still struggling with self-image, anxiety, and insecurities, Aimee felt out of place as a pastor's wife. With the birth of their first child, because the new church job did not provide medical insurance, Aimee continued working, further isolating her from the stay-at-home moms in the congregation. Then, when her new baby developed health issues, Aimee's isolation and fears resulted in depression.

Motherhood only increased Aimee's anxiety level. Aimee feared her kids would get sick, fail, or that she might die and leave them motherless. Because her husband was busy with his new job and worked many evenings, and she worked during the day outside the home, she felt like a single parent, so tired and alone. "I vividly remember with each child, feeding them late at night, feeling exhausted and fearful of the dark. I'd gaze at them and feel a sense of sadness and loneliness."

During those black nights, Aimee clung to verses about God's light in her darkness. What seems obvious now—but undiagnosed at the time—was that she suffered from post-partum depression. But despite the darkness, Aimee realized she was not alone and that God had glorious days of light ahead. Though becoming a mother heightened Aimee's anxieties, it also deepened her trust and her need to look to the

Lord as her strength. "Now that my children are older, when I'm up late worrying because they're sick, I remember a cozy sense of warmth and light, and I thank God."

With 20/20 hindsight, Aimee sheds further light on her perspective.

1. Understand that time goes by so quickly; don't wish it away.
2. Accept your strengths and weaknesses. She exclaims, "I am a work in progress and my kids love and accept me for that."
3. Realize you will enjoy some stages of mothering more than others. It's OK not to love crafts, pretend play on the floor, or making Christmas cookies from scratch.
4. Ask for wisdom from Christian friends who help you NOT filter your motherhood experience through fear.

"Being a mom has been rewarding and stretching, and the best thing I've ever done," Aimee said. That's strong reassurance for all of us! But it's also helpful to hear that whether giving birth, adopting, or becoming a stepmother, there will be times of disappointment, anxiety, or depression. These periods are normal, and common. Don't be afraid to seek counsel and medical attention.

Because I (Ann) have a history of obsessive-compulsive disorder (OCD) and my mother suffered from post-partum depression (PPD), I wondered how I'd react when my first child was born. Though I didn't suffer from PPD, it helped to know there were resources and caring individuals who could help.

Sometimes getting out of a one- or two-day blue funk is as simple as breaking your routine. If you find yourself down for just a day or two, try eating a square meal with four colorful foods on your plate; go for a good walk or swim; luxuriate in a bubble bath while reading a good novel; or share with a close friend how you're feeling and what you are going through. Draw close to God, pray the Psalms, and sing hymns out loud.

But when it extends longer than a few days, do something more. Although Scripture brings light and life, depression can be biologically based—not circumstantially based, and it is not a "failure of faith" if Christians seek help. Emotional challenges can happen at any stage of parenting. Be aware of resources, counselors, or doctors who can help you through depression and anxiety. PPD and persistent sadness and depression are treatable conditions. Psychotherapy alone helps some people, while others require medication. Treating depression keeps it from becoming a lingering problem that can affect you and your entire family long-term.

And if you've never struggled with depression or anxiety, could it be that you might need to be more aware of others who have? Could it be that somebody like Aimee might be misjudged as "having it altogether"? Or maybe thought of as aloof or unfriendly when she might be insecure and unhappy? The Lord calls us not to judge but to pray for one another, and to reach out with the comfort He has given us. How can you bring light to someone who is struggling?

Heartwork

Aimee learned to claim verses. Start collecting and storing up verses like Psalms 121:7: "The LORD will keep you from all harm—he will watch over your life." And for times of darkness, read aloud verses of light. Feel His presence and His light and love. Understand who God is and the truth of His love and strength.

Today, read aloud the following verses (the word "light" is bolded throughout):

> *You, O LORD, keep my lamp burning; my God turns my darkness into **light**. (Psalms 18:28)*
>
> *The LORD is my **light** and my salvation—whom shall I fear? The LORD is the stronghold of my life—of whom shall I be afraid? (Psalms 27:1)*
>
> *You are resplendent with **light**, more majestic than mountains rich with game. (Psalms 76:4)*
>
> *Blessed are those who have learned to acclaim you, who walk in the **light** of your presence, O LORD. (Psalms 89:15)*
>
> *. . . The LORD will be your everlasting **light**, and your God will be your glory. (Isaiah 60:19)*
>
> *"For God, who said, "Let **light** shine out of darkness,"*

*made his **light** shine in our hearts to give us the **light** of the knowledge of the glory of God in the face of Christ. (2 Corinthians 4:6)*

*This is the message we have heard from him and declare to you: God is **light**; in him there is no darkness at all. (1 John 1:5)*

In fact, we receive forgiveness of sins and the knowledge of salvation through the tender mercy of our God, "by which the rising sun will come to us from heaven to shine on those living in darkness and in the shadow of death, to guide our feet into the path of peace." (Luke 1:78–79)

God doesn't want His people to live in darkness and without salvation, but He doesn't want us to be under any other forms of darkness either. That's why He came to earth in the first place! Light reveals God to man. It is through Jesus that we can see God. Jesus says in John 12:46, "I have come into the world as a **light**, so that no one who believes in me should stay in darkness" (emphasis added).

Jesus makes seven different "I Am" claims in John. The second one is, "I am the **light** of the world. Whoever follows me will never walk in darkness, but will have the **light** of life." (John 8:12, emphasis added).

1. Why do you think Jesus calls Himself the "light of the world"? Since Jesus is the light of the world, how can He light up your life?

_____

_____

_____

2. First Peter 2:9 reminds us that we are called out of darkness and into His wonderful light. What is our responsibility according to 1 Peter 2:9?

*But you are a chosen people, a royal priesthood, a holy nation, a people belonging to God, that you may declare the praises of him who called you out of darkness into his wonderful **light**.*

_____

_____

_____

3. Read Psalms 139:1–16 below. Try reading it as a prayer.

> *O Lord, you have searched me and you know me. You know when I sit and when I rise; you perceive my thoughts from afar. You discern my going out and my lying down; you are familiar with all my ways. Before a word is on my tongue you know it completely, O Lord. You hem me in—behind and before; you have laid your hand upon me. Such knowledge is too wonderful for me, too lofty for me to attain.*
>
> *Where can I go from your Spirit? Where can I flee from your presence?*
>
> *If I go up to the heavens, you are there; if I make my bed in the depths, you are there. If I rise on the wings of the dawn, if I settle on the far side of the sea, even there your hand will guide me, your right hand will hold me fast.*
>
> *If I say, "Surely the darkness will hide me and the light become night around me," even the darkness will not be dark to you; the night will shine like the day, for darkness is as light to you.*
>
> *For you created my inmost being; you knit me together in my mother's womb.*
>
> *I praise you because I am fearfully and wonderfully made; your works are wonderful, I know that full well.*
>
> *My frame was not hidden from you when I was made in the secret place. When I was woven together in the depths of the earth, your eyes saw my unformed body. All the days ordained for me were written in your book before one of them came to be.*

4. How do the verses above bring you confidence as a parent?

_____

_____

_____

5. Find one phrase from the verses above that bring you a sense of calm, and then underline it.

The Psalms are laden with praise. Praise helps us consider how BIG God is and recognize His power and majesty.

Response: For our closing prayer, read Psalms 43:3–5 aloud, putting your confidence in Him.

*O L*ORD*, Send forth your light and your truth, let them guide me; let them bring me to your holy mountain, to the place where you dwell. Then will I go to the altar of God, to God, my joy and my delight. I will praise you with the harp, O God, my God. Why are you downcast, O my soul? Why so disturbed within me? Put your hope in God, for I will yet praise him, my Savior and my God.*

Jane always wanted children but never dreamt it was possible. In her forties and her second marriage, she went through testing, but the source of the problem was unclear. I always knew Jane would be a good mom. She loved to watch my two daughters, was a strong believer, and everybody came to her for counsel. But the clincher was when she came over one evening and my three-year-old threw up all over my husband. Jane didn't bat an eye; she still sat down and ate dinner. But what Jane had to learn was that she needed to lower her expectations; she would never be the perfect Mom she always thought she could be.

> *Sons are a heritage from the L*ORD*, children a reward from him. (Psalm 127:3)*

An Open Heart... Unwraps Gifts—Jane   *Day Five*

As Jane and her husband pursued adopting an older child, a relative of Jane's lost custody of her two-year-old daughter and three-year-old son and wanted Jane and her husband to adopt them. The soon-to-be-parents could hardly wait to fly from Virginia to Texas to meet these children and take them home. But how would the kids react?

All the way there on the plane, and then traveling forty-five minutes to the foster home, I rehearsed what I wanted to say. How I was going to tell them, playing over and over how they will react (will they cry, be afraid, or just disinterested in the whole ordeal?), and finally I see them in the flesh (no more pictures to go by) and my heart is so full, ready to burst with excitement and relief. Then the first words I hear from my daughter's mouth are "Mommy" as she runs to my lap—lots of tears, tears of joy. I felt so overwhelmed at that moment that words could not even describe the feelings. —*Jane*

Her two-year-old daughter sat on her lap the entire time, and Jane never wanted to let her go again. "I wanted to give her so much, and my new son, too. Then came the reality of 'Wow, I am now responsible for these little lives.' A roller coaster of emotions, but one worth taking."

Jane was emotional, but she didn't know how much more emotional it would get being peri-menopausal with preschoolers! Her daughter had been abandoned and mistreated; her son had been over-medicated because of an incorrect diagnosis. Jane and her husband had to sort out the problems and quickly learn how to create a warm and safe home for all four of them.

Initially, they set themselves apart from the outside world and focused on their new life together in their little home in the woods.

At first, Jane tried to make up for what the kids didn't get in their early years.

> I still can't stop smiling when I think of our first meeting and even now, when I check on them at night and watch them sleep, I get chills and this warm feeling of how truly blessed I am to have both of my children.

Having started out late, in my mid-forties, I thought I had it all together. My house was in order; things were lined up, and I had more wisdom over the young mothers (so I thought). I thought I could pretty much be a perfect mom. No one ever told me that perfection could never be reached. There is no such thing as a perfect mother. I was really hard on myself in the beginning, trying to be the June Cleaver of our day. —*Jane*

Now Jane realizes that only through God can she be the mother He wants her to be.

> God has gotten me through parenting this far and He will take me the rest of the way. It is His strength I lean on those days that just wipe me out, it is His wisdom that helps me solve even the smallest problems. (Where do all the socks really go?) It is God's faith in me to be a mom that encourages me to keep going (after all, He placed two beautiful children in my life because He knew I would take care of them). But most of all it is God's love that blesses me as a mom and allows me to bless my children. I wish someone would have told me that. —*Jane*

Jane reflected on three gifts Motherhood has brought her. Open her three gifts and think about them in your Heartwork.

Heartwork: The Gift of Bonding

Jane said,

> I was immediately drawn to Matthew 19:14 where Jesus said, 'Let the little children come to me, and do not hinder them for the kingdom of heaven belongs to such as these.' Jesus always made children a priority, even telling the disciples who were trying to keep the children from bothering him to let them come. Nothing was more important to Him then spending time with the children and bonding with them, no matter what His schedule looked like. That's what I want to always remember to say to my children—let them come.
>
> I wish someone had told me to pace myself and not to sweat the small stuff. My housework was no longer my priority. Time spent with my children became the most important thing for me. Teaching them, giving them a safe haven, and mostly just loving them and sitting and reading together. They needed the bonding, and believe it or not, so did I. —*Jane*

> "Jesus said, 'Let the little children come to me, and do not hinder them for the kingdom of heaven belongs to such as these.'"
> (Matthew 19:14)

Now consider three passages from three different Gospel writers about Jesus' response to children.

> *Then little children were brought to Jesus for him to place his hands on them and pray for them. But the disciples rebuked those who brought them.*
>
> *Jesus said, "Let the little children come to me, and do not hinder them, for the kingdom of heaven belongs to such as these." When he had placed his hands on them, he went on from there. (Matthew 19:13–15)*

> *People were bringing little children to Jesus to have him touch them, but the disciples rebuked them. When Jesus saw this, he was indignant. He said to them, "Let the little children come to me, and do not hinder them, for the kingdom of God belongs to such as these. I tell you the truth, anyone who will not receive the kingdom of God like a little child will never enter it." And he took the children in his arms, put his hands on them and blessed them. (Mark 10:13–16)*

> *People were also bringing babies to Jesus to have him touch them. When the disciples saw this, they rebuked them. But Jesus called the children to him and said, "Let the little children come to me, and do not hinder them, for the kingdom of God belongs to such as these. I tell you the truth, anyone who will not receive the kingdom of God like a little child will never enter it." (Luke 18:15–17)*

1. What did Jesus do when people brought children to Him?

_____

_____

_____

2. What do Jesus' actions teach you about the way to treat your children? What priority does Jesus place on children?

_____

_____

_____

The arrival of children can cause you to re-examine your relationship with God and others, and it can also make you re-evaluate your marriage. Sometimes pride or self-image gets in the way. And though Jane is an accomplished actress, it wasn't her background in drama that made her make a scene in front of her preschoolers.

The Gift of Help

I also wish someone had told me it's okay to admit you are struggling and ask for prayer. It doesn't mean you are a bad mom—just the opposite. Mothers who don't care wouldn't even think about how they were interacting with their children. One of my greatest moves was admitting to my close friends and family that I was floundering and needed their prayers and wisdom to get me through the toddler phase. I believe that's why God gave us friends, so we can lean on one another and help each other through these growing years with our children. —*Jane*

3. Friends will help you grow as a mother. The following two passages from Psalms and Proverbs describe, in a unique way, the "kindness" of a friend. What can you learn from them?

_____

_____

_____

Wounds from a friend can be trusted, but an enemy multiplies kisses. (Proverbs 27:6)

Let a righteous man strike me—it is a kindness; let him rebuke me—it is oil on my head. My head will not refuse it. Yet my prayer is ever against the deeds of evildoers. (Psalms 141:5)

4. The "wounds" of Proverbs 27:6 are called a "kindness" in Psalms 141:5. Could you accept "wounds" from a friend if they were "kindnesses"? In other words, are you ready to hear helpful suggestions from someone you trust?

_____

_____

_____

5. List three friends you can trust or three mothers whose parenting skills you admire. In what ways can you further develop relationships with these women?

_____

_____

_____

> ❧ wouldn't have made it but for my friends and family and being able to trust them with some rather tender areas in my life as a mom and wife. Knowing they were praying me through was a huge comfort during those difficult times.
> —Jane

6. How can you prepare even now, to humbly accept comments, encouragement, and consolation from respected friends?

_____

_____

_____

Jane not only found her solace in her friends and family; like so many moms, she reiterated the need for prayer.

The Gift of God's Trust and Love for Me

I wish someone had told me to buy a pair of knee pads. Because with children, I find I'm on my knees praying more than I ever have before. When they are sick, I pray for them; when they have a bad day, I pray for them; when I have a bad day, I pray for them; when I feel I have failed or just don't know what I should be doing to give them the most of what I can in an area where they need it, I pray for them.

> "I prayed for this child, and the LORD has granted me what I asked of him."
> (1 Samuel 1:27)

If wanting to be a good mom to your children doesn't bring you to your knees on occasion, or in my case, a lot, then I don't know who else you could turn to. Hannah was blessed with the gift of a child, and God has so greatly blessed my husband and me with the gift of two children—all in answer to our many prayers. —*Jane*

7. What about you? Did you pray for your child? Consider Hannah. She prayed for Samuel and dedicated his life to God. How will you begin a life of prayer for your child?

_____

_____

_____

8. If you need a little help, pray these verses that bring Jane comfort, protection, and wisdom as she begins each day. Write this passage on a note card and put it on your bathroom mirror until you have it memorized.

Let the morning bring me word of your unfailing love, for I have put my trust in you. Show me the way I should go, for to you I lift up my soul. Rescue me from my enemies, O LORD, for I hide myself in you. Teach me to do your will, for you are my God; may your good Spirit lead me on level ground. (Psalms 143:8–10)

Response: *Lord, You are wise and all-knowing. You know the children I am to raise. Forgive me for the times I have not given children the love and respect you show them. Please help me listen to the kindnesses of my friends and to bond with my children as I put my trust in You. Thank you for entrusting me with my children, and for choosing us for each other. Help me to continually pray for my children.*

> *Being a mom is a true blessing. Your children are a gift, and you need to cherish them and love them. God will take care of the rest.* —Jane

A Full Heart

Hopefully, this week you close with a full heart spilling over with treasures for your children. You will meet Jodie, Karen, Ann, Xandra, and Rachelle who will remind you to love, celebrate, guard your heart, and teach and pray from the Word.

A Full Heart . . .

Loves—Jodie
Celebrates—Karen
Listens and Speaks—Ann
Teaches—Xandra
Prays the Word—Rachelle

Jodie's friends and family know her as the inventor of "positive payoff." She can turn drudgery into fun because she looks for the silver lining. She inserts picnics and parks in the middle of errand running. But ultimately, she knows what's most important—love. Her parenting motto is: "Every child needs to know he or she is safe and loved."

*We **love** because he first loved us.* (1 John 4:19)

*I have loved you with an everlasting **love**; I have drawn you with loving-kindness.* (Jeremiah 31:3)

Day One
A Full Heart... Loves—Jodie

Andy and Jodie are the parents of three very active daughters: Megan, Morgan, and Mallory. Early in their parenting, Andy and Jodie both worked full-time, and life seemed chaotic. Marital strife, tension, dependence on other caretakers, and even a separation strained their family. Though Jodie felt called to stay at home, she knew it would mean serious lifestyle changes. Knowing no one could love her children like she did, she quit her job to become a stay-at-home mom. They sold their large home, moved hundreds of miles away to a less expensive area of the state, purchased a smaller home, and made other significant adjustments.

After a few years of stability and comfort, Andy and Jodie both realized Andy needed to pursue his dream: teaching history and coaching high school football. Jodie would have to *return* to work so Andy could *return* to school. Jodie sacrificed and made her marriage, as well as her children, a priority.

Has it been easy? No. Five family members with differing schedules and goals don't all realize their dreams. In fact, they've all made a lot of challenging sacrifices. Still Jodie keeps her motto: Children need to feel safe and loved. A part of that security is time. "What children need most is *time* with their parents—both *quantity* and *quality*."

Jodie has not always found her personal positive payoff. But love trusts, hopes, perseveres, and never fails (1 Corinthians 13). And parenting is a process of practicing the second most important commandment: "Love one another."

In theory it sounds so simple, but in practice it's a challenge because so many things can happen in a day that make you angry, frustrated, impatient, and jealous. Too often, you may not love in the selfless and sacrificial way Christ loved you. And so today, focus on what scripture says about love.

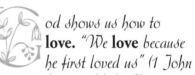

od shows us how to **love.** *"We* **love** *because he first loved us" (1 John 4:19, emphasis added). Our example shows our children how to love. In meeting our children's physical needs, mothers lay a foundation for a lifetime of spiritual growth for their children.* **–Anita**

Heartwork

1. What do the following verses teach you about the greatest motivator to walk in truth?

> *Test me, O LORD, and try me, examine my heart and my mind; for your love is ever before me, and I walk continually in your truth. (Psalms 26:2–3)*

*Teach me your way, O LORD, and I will walk in your truth; give me an undivided heart, that I may fear your name. I will praise you, O LORD my God, with all my heart; I will glorify your name forever. **For great is your love toward me** (Psalms 86:11–13a, emphasis added)*

_____

_____

_____

2. The following verses (with emphasis added) further teach about love. As you read each verse, write something you've learned in the love tank column, and if you can, how that kind of love would be acted out in your family.

_____

_____

_____

> *alling to mind what Jesus proclaimed to be the two greatest commandments, we know that the best gift we can give our children besides the knowledge of a loving Savior is the gift of our own love. Give time to the biblical study of what exactly it means to love one another and more specifically, to love and discipline our children. —Barb B.*

Verses:

*Be imitators of God, therefore, as dearly loved children and live a life of **love**, just as Christ loved us and gave himself up for us as a fragrant offering and sacrifice to God.* (Ephesians 5:1–2)

*And this is **love**: that we walk in obedience to his commands. As you have heard from the beginning, his command is that you walk in **love**.* (2 John 6)

*As the Father has loved me, so have I loved you. Now remain in my **love**. If you obey my commands, you will remain in my **love**, just as I have obeyed my Father's commands and remain in his **love**. My command is this: **Love** each other as I have loved you. Greater **love** has no one than this, that he lay down his life for his friends. This is my command: **Love** each other.* (John 15:9–17)

*Dear friends, let us **love** one another, for **love** comes from God. Everyone who loves has been born of God and knows God.*

*Whoever does not **love** does not know God, because God is **love.***

*This is how God showed his **love** among us: He sent his one and only Son into the world that we might live through him.*

*This is **love**: not that we loved God, but that he loved us and sent his Son as an atoning sacrifice for our sins.*

*Dear friends, since God so loved us, we also ought to **love** one another.* (1 John 4:7–11)

Love Tank:

2. Consider your role as a wife or mom as you read the following scriptures. Do your well-meaning actions ever *fail* to demonstrate love? On the line below each of the verses, re-rewrite the phrase in your own words and with your own life situations. I've done the first two for myself . . . ouch!

How to be a Big Zero from 1 Corinthians 13

*If I speak in the tongues of men and of angels, but have not **love**, I am only a resounding gong or a clanging cymbal. (verse 1)*

(If I write a Bible study on motherhood, and lead my daughters' after-school discipleship group, but don't have time to read them a bedtime story, my faith will ring false to them.)

_____

_____

_____

*If I have the gift of prophecy and can fathom all mysteries and all knowledge, and if I have a faith that can move mountains, but have not **love**, I am nothing. (verse 2)*

(If I pray on the prayer chain, counsel needy friends, and take a meal to someone in need, but don't encourage my husband or share a loving touch, I will not be speaking his love language and my faith may be a turn-off.)

_____

_____

_____

*If I give all I possess to the poor and surrender my body to the flames, but have not **love**, I gain nothing. (verse 3)*

_____

_____

_____

_____

This is Love:

     Love _is patient,_ **_love_** _is kind. It does not envy, it does not boast, it is not proud. (verse 4)_

_____

_____

_____

     It is not rude, it is not self-seeking, it is not easily angered, it keeps no record of wrongs. (verse 5)

_____

_____

_____

     Love _does not delight in evil but rejoices with the truth. (verse 6)_

_____

_____

_____

     It always protects, always trusts, always hopes, always perseveres. (verse 7)

_____

_____

_____

     Love _never fails. (verse 8)_

_____

_____

_____

(And just in case you didn't get the idea . . .)

*And now these three remain: faith, hope and **love**.*
*But the greatest of these is **love**. (verse 13)*

3. First John 3:18 says, "Dear children, let us not **love** with words or tongue but with actions and in truth." What does it mean to love with *actions and in truth*? What would that kind of love look like?

_____

_____

_____

"The only thing that counts is faith expressing itself through **love**."
(Galatians 5:6b)

4. Revisit the passage you read about what to "put on"; but this time, focus on the powerful side effects of love.

*Therefore, as God's chosen people, holy and dearly loved, clothe yourselves with compassion, kindness, humility, gentleness and patience. Bear with each other and forgive whatever grievances you may have against one another. Forgive as the Lord forgave you. And over all these virtues put on **love**, which binds them all together in perfect unity. (Colossians 3:12–14, emphasis added)*

Think about your home. What does your love do to kindness, humility, gentleness, patience, and forgiveness? Read that last sentence again and write what love does.

Love _____ _____ ___ _____ ___
_____ _____.

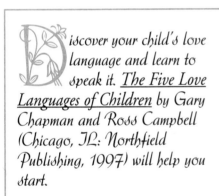

Discover your child's love language and learn to speak it. <u>The Five Love Languages of Children</u> by Gary Chapman and Ross Campbell (Chicago, IL: Northfield Publishing, 1997) will help you start.

Response: *Lord, Your words say, "And now these three remain: faith, hope and love. But the greatest of these is love." Your words say love is the most important link. Fill my home with love. Help me pay attention to the information in the love tank and imitate Your love, and look to Your scriptures for how to demonstrate love to my family.*

R38

Recently, in the shopping mall, I saw moms pushing strollers and remembered when that was me. For a moment I longed to recapture my kids at that age: what they sounded like, looked like, and (for the most part) smelled like. And I wanted one of those days to do over. I wondered, "Did we *enjoy* every day as much as we could have? Did we take *joy* in the journey?"

As a mom, one day you may receive a precious handprint made by your child with a little verse saying, "Don't mind my messes. One day I'll be all grown up and you'll miss me." This yanks on heart strings like nothing else, and you'll vow to celebrate each little moment and not get frustrated when your baby/toddler/preschooler/pre-teen does something frustrating. But the bottom line is, you can't completely fulfill your vow to live in the moment, because you don't yet have the full perspective of a lifetime of moments. If you did, you'd probably long to go back and re-parent certain ages—with the right priorities.

But since you can't, you need to learn to celebrate each special moment, each day, and each stage as it comes. And always take joy in the journey.

> *This is the day the LORD has made; let us rejoice and be glad in it. (Psalms 118:24)*

A Full Heart... Celebrates—Karen

My friend Karen lives in a farmhouse near the small town of Waterford. Because her house isn't completely finished according to her dreams, she is relaxed in how she lets her children play. Chalk drawings decorate the front steps leading into her two-story home. The grand living room is filled with children's toys. On any given day, Karen and the kids are building tents or creating a fort out of cardboard boxes and having picnics in the living room. They move outdoors to play in the rain, fly kites, or go on nature walks to collect treasures. The treasures include grass and a few caterpillars to take residence in the indoor dollhouse. Summer days extend into evenings with bonfires, roasting marshmallows, and maybe even campouts. Karen and her kids stop to see a beautiful sunrise, sunset, full moon, or a rainbow.

Her advice to new moms? To "Get ready to be a kid again and play! Be spontaneous to your kids' requests. Don't let dolls sit on the shelf. If you don't want something scratched, put it in storage. While you're at it, put the TV in storage too."

> The future is what we do today—all of our mundane todays will make up our children's lives. It's the dozens of little things we do every day that matter—a tone of voice, a look in the eye, a kind, or unkind word. Be ready to let the dishes, the laundry, and the dust bunnies pile up so you can spend family time with your kids. They will remember your time with them, not how clean the house is (or what toys you bought them). —*Karen*

Though a perfect home should not become your idol, balance and boundaries are necessary. Your home will function better with a sense of order and children sharing in the housework. And chores can be a fun predecessor to play.

Karen encourages joy through celebration and play:

> When the kids were smaller, they loved it when I held them and danced around the house to the music. We'd twirl and step to a waltz or whatever. It was especially easy to run and dance in the living room back then because we had so little furniture—only a couch and a coffee table!

Karen quoted the verse about how the Israelites celebrated when the Lord brought the captives back to Zion.

> *We were like men who dreamed. Our mouths were filled with laughter, our tongues with songs of joy. Then it was said among the nations, "The LORD has done great things for them." The LORD has done great things for us, and we are filled with joy. (Psalms 126:1–3)*

"And we are filled with joy. . . . " Can *your* house be filled with joy? There is a time for everything—especially joy! Is your house filled with joy? What can you do to foster joy in your home?

*There is a time for everything, and a season for every activity under heaven (Ecclesiastes 3:1). . . . a time to weep and **a time to laugh**, a time to mourn and **a time to dance.** (verse 4)*

The Israelites commemorated special times and harvests. They celebrated the Feast of Unleavened Bread, Feast of First Fruits, Feast of Weeks, Feast of Trumpets, and Feast of Tabernacles. What a beautiful example to follow. They gathered together for fellowship, food, and rejoicing. What about you? How can you learn to rejoice in today? How can you celebrate not only *milestones*, but *moments*?

Though this is not meant to be an idea book with lists of things to do, I want to share a few ideas to get you thinking about the celebration of life.

Post a calendar in your baby's bedroom. Note the milestones of development.

Annually celebrate your child's baptism and the day he/she accepted Jesus.

My Aunt Lydia celebrates God's will. When her children were young and ran for a position in school government or tried out for a play or team, the family prayed about the process. On the day of the decision, she planned a "Celebration of God's Will." And when the kids came home with the results, they celebrated—win or lose.

Family Life Ministries offers a practical packet entitled "Passport to Purity," which is a wonderful way to tell your children about the birds and the bees. A parent and child go away for a night or two and have a rewarding and bonding weekend. It's a milestone in the child and parent's life.

Dannah Gresh wrote a book entitled *Secret Keeper Girl Kit: Great Dates for You and Your Daughter* (Chicago, IL: Moody Publishers, 2004). Each date is a mini-celebration that reinforces modesty, purity, and teaches biblical sexuality.

Heartwork

You can turn the ordinary into the *extra*ordinary by seeing God's fingerprints. When a rainbow appears in the sky, you can point it out and say, "Thank you, God, for rainbows!" and help others see His handiwork. You can also **bring joy** through simple celebrations. Light a candle at dinner, smile at everyone you see at the mall, or play Dad's favorite song when he walks in the door.

So how do you learn to live in the moment? One way is to listen to the wisdom of older friends and relatives who have gone before, who tell you to relax and "smell the roses." Then you can **take joy in the *journey*** instead of in the *destination.* Joy along the way lets you appreciate smaller moments so you won't stress out about whether you'll arrive at your target. If you have the perspective to celebrate the little moments, you will **look for joy.**

God is the author of joy. Over and over Jesus states He wants your joy to be complete by remaining in His love and obeying His commands (John 15:9–11).

My sister-in-law, Caroline, is a planner. When she had her third and last child, she realized she needed to stop and experience every part of little Katie's growth.

Although we want to parent with a long-term goal in mind, we also need to remember to live in the moment. Be present with your children. Watch their expressions. Inhale their scent. Listen to their babble. Delight in what they see. Feel the texture of their hair. Let time stand still and drink in the beauty of God through your children's eyes. God is the great I AM—the God of the moment. Watch for him in your kids. When you serve your children like you're serving Jesus you will be delighted to find He has satisfied your heart. —*Caroline*

> *If you look, you'll find a little tiny piece of joy flying around every day. Some days it's a friend who says or does just the right thing. Other days, it's the shape of your baby's little toes, the murmur of contented children, the tree outside your window, the sound of the school bus, a comment from a stranger, a smile. Find it, grab it, and treasure it—it's your little pick me up from God. –Marci*

> "If you have any encouragement from being united with Christ, if any comfort from his love, if any fellowship with the Spirit, if any tenderness and compassion, then make my joy complete by being like-minded, having the same love, being one in spirit and purpose."
>
> (Philippians 2:1–2)

1. Try listing ways to celebrate with your senses:

Tasting _____

Touching _____

Hearing _____

Smelling_____

Seeing_____

2. List a few ages and stages you might want to celebrate with your children. (You can even include the first gray hair!) "Gray hair is a crown of splendor; it is attained by a righteous life" (Proverbs 16:31). "The glory of young men is their strength, gray hair the splendor of the old" (Proverbs 20:29).

_____

_____

_____

3. Doodle a list of things or draw a few sketches of things that simply make you happy:

_____

_____

_____

Celebrate God's goodness in all things big and small, good and bad. Celebrate out loud! —Kim

4. Jot down a few ideas of how to remind yourself to celebrate the seconds of your life and not just the big moments.

_____

_____

_____

Choose joy each day. On mornings when we're late and miss the bus, sometimes my girls and I have trouble feeling joyful. We're all crabby on the drive to school, and so we break into song, "*This is the day which the Lord has made,*" and we rejoice and are glad in it (Psalms 118:24). Notice the verse says, "This is the *day.*" It could have been this is the *week* or the *month* or the *year,* but maybe that would have seemed overwhelming and unmanageable. We can handle one day at a time. Sometimes my husband asks me, "What kind of day are you going to have?" He reminds me I can decide to have a *good* day, a day to *rejoice.*

And when you're not sure you have anything to feel joyful about, consider Psalms 31:7 and say, "I am radiant with joy because of your mercy, for you have listened to my troubles and have seen the crisis in my soul." This verse can remind you to experience joy because God sees your needs and understands your sorrow. You can also **consider it joy** when you understand that trials test your faith, leading to perseverance and to maturing! Your children will mature when they encounter testing. Hang on to God, and consider it all joy. And remember, joy is not happiness. It is decision of the soul to believe God has our good in mind.

> *Consider it pure joy, my brothers, whenever you face trials of many kinds, because you know that the testing of your faith develops perseverance. Perseverance must finish its work so that you may be mature and complete, not lacking anything. (James 1:2–4)*

5. **Sing for joy.** Write down a list of happy songs to sing unto the Lord. He likes to hear them, and you'll become happier by singing them. "Sing to the LORD a new song; sing to the LORD, all the earth." (Psalms 96:1)

_____

_____

_____

_____

6. Using these verses, what can you learn about celebration and praise and add to your joy tank? (Joy Tank chart on next page)

When I think of the possibilities for joy, I get excited and want to try them out. What child wouldn't be more content celebrating each day?

Response: *Lord, please give me a contented heart that overflows with thanksgiving and joy. Let me find my joy in You and Your creation. Let the joy You supply overflow into the lives of others, so they, too, will joyfully rejoice in everything.*

What flows from our hearts comes out of our mouths. And the words of our mouths set the tone in our homes. We know an apt word spoken at the right time offers encouragement. And yet, every mom regrets things she has said to her child,

Joy Verses

Joy Tank

I will praise you, O LORD, with all my heart; I will tell of all your wonders. I will be glad and rejoice in you; I will sing praise to your name, O Most High. (Psalms 9:1–2)

Our mouths were filled with laughter, our tongues with songs of joy. Then it was said among the nations, "The LORD has done great things for them." (Psalms 126:2)

May the God of hope fill you with all joy and peace as you trust in him, so that you may overflow with hope by the power of the Holy Spirit. (Romans 15:13)

He will yet fill your mouth with laughter and your lips with shouts of joy. (Job 8:21)

Shout for joy to the LORD, all the earth. Worship the LORD with gladness; come before him with joyful songs. (Psalms 100:1–2)

The LORD has done great things for us, and we are filled with joy. (Psalms 126:3)

Speak to one another with psalms, hymns and spiritual songs. Sing and make music in your heart to the Lord, always giving thanks to God the Father for everything, in the name of our Lord Jesus Christ (Ephesians 5:19–20).

and some time or another goes to bed reviewing hasty words and worrying how she's hurt her child's feelings.

> *Do not let any unwholesome talk come out of your mouths, but only what is helpful for building others up according to their needs, that it may benefit those who listen. (Ephesians 4:29)*

Day Three   A Full Heart... Listens and Speaks—Ann

This is not the day I should be talking. Literally. I'm a storyteller who likes to talk more than listen. I work out my thoughts by venting, and at times I don't do it in the most appropriate way. I don't take enough time before I speak to my children. Sometimes my speech grade on my report card would be, "Needs Improvement." But I also know that speech encourages, and I've seen the power of positive communication. That's what we'll look at today.

"We who are strong ought to bear with the failings of the weak and not to please ourselves. Each of us should please his neighbor for his good, to build him up."
(Romans 15:1–2)

Do our words express encouragement and love? Do we refrain from criticism and gossip? Even now, we can begin to practice refraining from words that tear down rather than build up. I have two beautiful daughters. When they sing and when they speak, I can hear my voice or my words. Sometimes their reflection reveals and convicts. Of course I delight when I hear them encourage one another and speak positively. And I know that it doesn't just please me, it pleases God.

What if we started each day with this prayer from Psalms 19:14? "May the words of my mouth and the meditation of my heart be pleasing in your sight, O LORD, my Rock and my Redeemer."

James cautions about the negative power of the tongue. James uses metaphors to explain that the tongue is like a bit in the mouth of the horse, a rudder on a ship, or a fire in the forest. It has great power and potential for damage (see James 3:3–6). He even says, "no man can tame the tongue. It is a restless evil, full of deadly poison" (verses 8–9). And to prove our duplicity, he adds, "With the tongue we praise our Lord and

Father, and with it we curse men, who have been made in God's likeness." Ouch! What a discouraging picture!

So what do we do about it? James offers a formula in verses 19 and 20:

> *My dear brothers, take note of this: Everyone should be **quick** to listen, **slow** to speak and **slow** to become angry, for man's anger does not bring about the righteous life that God desires. (emphasis added)*

My daughters and I drew pictures of QUICK, SLOW, SLOW in our Bible journals. It helped create a mental picture of what to consider before speaking. Julia's drawing features a girl driving a car saying "Quick to Listen" and a snail scooting alongside saying "S . . . L . . . O . . . W to Speak . . ." Christine's artsy picture depicts a "SLOW" traffic sign followed by "–2–Speak" and "SLOW–2–Anger", with the letters in *Anger* featured in a menacing looking font. I especially love Julia's depiction of Psalm 4:4, which shows one girl in bed saying "I'm mad at you Julia and the other girl saying, "I'm more mad at you" with a big X across the drawing! What a way to capture "In your anger do not sin; when you are on your beds search your hearts and be silent" (Psalms 4:4). By the way, as kids learn scripture, a great way to help visualize it is for them to draw it out—even if they can't write the words! A picture is worth a thousand words. As they grow older they can write the words and illustrate them. This journal becomes their own personal book of treasures from God's Word. I love to look at their understanding of God's Word and am thankful they are internalizing it.

Heartwork:

1. What could you do to help you remember to be *quick to listen, slow to speak, and slow to anger?*

_____

_____

_____

(One group suggested the following: Count to five before speaking, pretend you don't have a mouth, don't formulate an answer while listening, and to really prevent hasty words—run to the bathroom!)

These verses show the power and danger of the tongue. But I find I'm more motivated by seeking the positive than avoiding the negative. So speak out and encourage!

2. Underline the positive effects of the tongue from the following verses:

_____

_____

_____

My mouth will speak words of wisdom; the utterance from my heart will give understanding. (Psalms 49:3)

An anxious heart weighs a man down, but a kind word cheers him up. (Proverbs 12:25)

A gentle answer turns away wrath, but a harsh word stirs up anger. (Proverbs 15:1)

A word aptly spoken is like apples of gold in settings of silver. (Proverbs 25:11)

She speaks with wisdom, and faithful instruction is on her tongue. (Proverbs 31:26)

Let your conversation be always full of grace, seasoned with salt, so that you may know how to answer everyone. (Colossians 4:6)

3. Could someone say the following about you?

Her kind words cheer me up and help me not to worry so much. She always has just the right words to say at the right time. Her gentle answers stop arguments. I seek out her opinion and really listen to her because she has so many good instructions and wisdom. She's like a counselor who helps me understand myself better.

_____

_____

_____

There is a direct correlation between listening and speaking. Think back to the verse *quick to listen, slow to speak.* If you think this is hard to live out prior to children, it only gets more difficult after children. But when we learn to be quick to listen and slow to speak, our children will enter a dialogue.

Will you be a mommy who hears and really *listens* to what your children say? Will they feel like talking to you? Sometimes when I should be hearing the heart of my child, I only want to get *my* point across and prove that I am *right*.

How to Talk So Kids Will Listen & Listen So Kids Will Talk, by Adele Faber and Elaine Mazlish, (Bloomington, IN: Collins Living, 1999) is a great book that encourages both sides to dialogue. We will need these gates of communication open for their entire lives.

My friend Becky advises,

> Take time to 'listen' to your kids even when it's inconvenient. I'm learning to not be shocked or judgmental when my daughter tells me things that are happening at school with friends, because then she'll just shut up and run off. Kelsey doesn't really pour her heart out much, but when she does, I always stop what I'm doing and listen to her.

Mothers of sons tell me the most important minutes of their son's day are revealed right before they go to bed. In a little girl's life, it seems to be in the first fifteen minutes off the school bus. That's when I hear about something hurtful, have the privilege of easing the pain, and can direct their thoughts back to Jesus. It's a wonderful time to exercise the power of positive speech and an opportunity to build up your children.

Response: *Lord, help me to be a woman who speaks wisdom and instruction. May my words bekind and cheer others up. Prepare my heart to bring a timely word and joy. Season my conversation with grace. Help me to be a good listener. May I be quick to listen and slow to speak. Do not let any unwholesome talk come out of my mouth, but only what is helpful for building others up according to their needs, that it may benefit those who listen* (Ephesians 4:29).

As much as I might love my children, God loves them more than I do. He's taught me that people matter to God, and it matters to Him that I teach this to my children. And He has taught me my children not only want me to be available, they need me to be available—even when they say they don't. —Elizabeth

Children need from their mothers—tenderness, gentleness, love, grace, mercy, and lots of time. Moms can build up their homes with peace and joy or tear them down. —Karen

R 38

Some women who long to be mothers have stable homes and much love to offer. But they are unmarried. They feel a calling to parent, but what can they do with that desire? Some teach school, others mentor youth, and some become single parents. But whether a single parent, widowed, divorced, or married, a mother needs to teach her children from the depth of her heart to love and follow Jesus.

Be joyful always, pray continually; give thanks in all circumstances, for this is God's will for you in Christ Jesus. (1 Thessalonians 5:16–18)

Day Four · A Full Heart... Teaches—Xandra

Xandra practiced patience and prayer as she waited for God's perfect will. As a thirty-five-year-old teacher, though she longed to be a mom, God had not brought a Christian man to marry her. This caused her to spend much time in prayer, asking for direction from the Lord. Though she read Proverbs 19:21, "*Many are the plans of a man's heart, but it is the Lord's purpose that prevails,*" she wondered, 'What was His purpose?' Xandra had taught high school and preschool and loved children. She felt her longings weren't just personal, but that the Lord was calling her to look at ways to mother a child. Eventually, Xandra chose to become a foster parent with the goal of adopting.

On September 11, 2006, Xandra became the foster mother of a blonde-haired, blue-eyed, three-year-old boy named Larson. She had expected to wait before earning the title of "Mom." But when he arrived suddenly and she, her mom, and Larson went shopping to pick up all the items a new mom doesn't have, she was surprised at what happened when she shopped with Larson. Their story follows:

"**Mommy**, we should get the Nemo ones. I like Nemo."
"You like Nemo?" I said, smiling in surprise at my new name.

"Yes, **Mommy**, so can we get those?" I looked up at my mom, and we were both crying."

One month later, as we said our nightly bedtime prayers, as usual we prayed for one another, grandma and grandpa, Classy our dog, and concluded with "everyone we love." Every night I told Larson how glad I was God had answered my prayer and brought him to me. But on this night after our "Amens," Larson whispered,

"Mommy, want to know something? I prayed for you."

I kissed his forehead and whispered back, "I know sweetheart, I prayed for you, too."

Larson shook his head and corrected me, "No, Mommy, before I lived here, I prayed for you to be my mommy."

"You did?" I asked in surprise. "That was a good prayer, wasn't it?" he said, cozying up to me.

"That was the best prayer I know of," I said.

"And God thought so, too, because he answered it with you, Mommy."

After almost two years together, Larson has grown four inches and Xandra has grown immeasurably. As the two move toward the final adoption process, Xandra continues to focus on the fact that God is in control of all things, and in all things she puts her trust in Him—especially as a single parent.

In Xandra's years of teaching she has heard kids from age two through the teenage years yell, "I hate you," but not necessarily mean it. When those moments occur, she knows a mother's strength must come from the Lord. The mother needs to remain joyful, give thanks, but also discipline her child. A Scripture passage that has taken on new life for Xandra since she became Larson's mother is Proverbs 3:11–12: "My son, do not despise the LORD's discipline and do not resent his rebuke, because the LORD disciplines those he loves, as a father the son he delights in."

Xandra remembers these verses when her son tells her she is "not nice" for sending him to time-out. She knows this is a time for resolve and discipline.

Though being a single parent is a challenge, having a strong support system helps. Xandra says, "Asking for help is not a sign of weakness." She is so grateful to family, friends, and her church family, who helped her by living out this verse, "Therefore encourage one another and build each other up, just as in fact you are doing" (1 Thessalonians 5:11). Not only is it important to ask for help; Xandra feels it's especially important for moms to take a time-out.

> "My son, if you accept my words and store up my commands within you, turning your ear to wisdom and applying your heart to understanding, and if you call out for insight and cry aloud for understanding, and if you look for it as for silver and search for it as for hidden treasure, then you will understand the fear of the LORD and find the knowledge of God."
> (Proverbs 2:1–5)

The Lord never expected moms to be perfect, just to do their best to follow Him. We are works in progress. Patience is one skill we need to work on each day of parenting. To do so, we need to feed our souls and take time out to regain focus. Especially as single moms. —*Xandra*

Ephesians 1:4–6 has also taken on new depth for Xandra. "I have something in common with my adopted son. I was chosen before the creation of the world and adopted by God just as my son was chosen by God and by me."

Heartwork

1. If you were given the following commands from Deuteronomy 11:18–19 (emphasis added), what would you ask?

_____

_____

_____

> **Fix** *these words of mine in your hearts and minds;* **tie** *them as symbols on your hands and bind them on your foreheads.* **Teach** *them to your children, talking about them when you sit at home and when you walk along the road, when you lie down and when you get up.* (Deuteronomy 11:18–19)

> "For He chose us in him. . . . He predestined us to be adopted as his children. . . ."
> (Ephesians 1:4–6)

Maybe you would ask, "What are *'these words'* that Moses is talking about?" To find the answer we need to go back and look at verses 11 and 13 and Deuteronomy 6:4–9, which states the commandments clearly:

> *Hear, O Israel:* **The Lord our God, the Lord is one. Love the Lord your God with all your heart and with all your soul and with all your strength.** *These commandments that I give you today are to be upon your hearts. Impress them on your children. Talk about them when you sit at home and when you walk along the road, when you lie down and when you get up. Tie them as symbols on your hands and bind them on your foreheads. Write them on the doorframes of your houses and on your gates. (emphasis added)*

2. In the previous passages, God uses the following action verbs to emphasize the importance of teaching our children: Fix, Tie, Teach, Impress. How can you put these verbs into action and teach these commandments? In what ways can you "write them on the doorframes of your houses"?

> "Love the Lord your God with all your heart and with all your soul and with all your strength. These commandments that I give you today are to be upon your hearts."
> (Deuteronomy 6:5–6)

_____

_____

_____

_____

3. We need to pass on the stories from the Bible as well as the stories of God's faithfulness in our lives. Deuteronomy 11:2 emphasizes the need to teach our children and to pass along our heritage of faith:

> *Remember today that your children were not the ones who saw and experienced the discipline of the Lord your God: his majesty, his mighty hand, his outstretched arm.*

If you do not have a legacy of faith to pass on, you can read the stories from God's Word and share what God has done in the lives of others. Begin journaling passages to pass along to your children. Show your children God's majesty, His mighty hand, and His outstretched arm. In addition, what older friends or relatives could share their journeys of faith with your child? Finally, teach your children to see the great things the Lord is doing right now in their lives. List any ideas below.

_____

_____

_____

4. What action step can you take today to begin this process?

_____

_____

_____

Training your children in the way they should go demands God's wisdom. You can count on Him to provide for you each day.

Proverbs 22:6 commands, "Train a child in the way he should go, and when he is old he will not turn from it." The Hebrew word for train (*chanak*) can include to dedicate, discipline, initiate into God's Word and perhaps to whet the appetite for a new taste. The Hebrew word translated "way" (*derek*) can be thought of as a road or journey, a mode or habit, a duty or moral action.

5. Using the definitions above, take Proverbs 22:6 and rewrite it in your own words.

_____

_____

_____

> *In Exodus, God gave the Israelites manna for that day. If they gathered more than one day's worth, it spoiled. As mothers we can depend on God each day for the wisdom, endurance, and guidance for **that day**. Then the next day, He will provide again.*
> *—Anita*

And finally, we cannot forget the importance of teaching children to love God and love others. In the New Testament, Jesus quotes the command to "*Love the Lord your God with all your heart and all your soul and with all your mind and with all your strength*" (Mark 12:30). Writers Matthew and Luke also include His teaching on this in their Gospels. (Luke 10:27, Matthew 22:37)

> *One of the teachers of the law came and heard them debating. Noticing that Jesus had given them a good answer, he asked him, "Of all the commandments, which is the most important?"*

"The most important one," answered Jesus, "is this: 'Hear, O Israel, the Lord our God, the Lord is one. Love the Lord your God with all your heart and with all your soul and with all your mind and with all your strength.' The second is this: 'Love your neighbor as yourself.' There is no commandment greater than these." (Mark 12:28–31)

Matthew 22:40 concludes, "All the Law and the Prophets hang on these two commandments." Indeed, if we loved God and our neighbors, all the other laws would fall into place and our children would truly be trained in the way they should go! Similarly, Jesus states what is now known to be the "Golden Rule." "So in everything, do to others what you would have them do to you, for this sums up the Law and the Prophets" (Matthew 7:12).

Quite simply: Love God, love others, and treat them the way you'd like to be treated. That about sums up today's lesson! Now you can close in prayer.

Response: *Lord, I love You, God, with all my heart, mind, soul, and strength. Help me to pass on my heritage of faith. Guide me to train my child in the way he should go. In our walks together, may I continually share Your Word, teaching my child about what You have done in the past, what You are doing in the present, and about our glorious future together with You. When my child lies down, I will teach him to pray. And tomorrow when we rise, I will begin the day with something from Your Word.*

My friend Rachelle celebrates life. With a lovely soprano voice and the last name of Knight, she's known as "Knightngale." Her personality sings through the day as she raises her teenagers and runs a business caring for handicapped people in her home.

It should have come as no surprise when she forwarded to me a delightful birthday announcement inviting all of Rachelle's former grade school friends from Minnesota, North Dakota, Michigan, and even Italy to celebrate her fiftieth birthday back home in Minnesota. As leader of the party pack, she chose a queen bee theme and labeled the rest of her forty-something friends as "Wanna-bees." She collected tiaras, scepters, and queenly attire for the big celebration.

What makes someone celebrate life to that degree? Perhaps it's a prayer life brimming with thankfulness and joy.

> *"And this is my prayer: that your love may abound more and more in knowledge and depth of insight, so that you may be able to discern what is best and may be pure and blameless until the day of Christ, filled with the fruit of righteousness that comes through Jesus Christ—to the glory and praise of God." (Philippians 1:9–11)*

Day Five — A Full Heart... Prays the Word—Rachelle

Carl remembers first being attracted to Rachelle when he heard her singing down the hall. They later married, forging ahead, not necessarily blessed by his black family or her white relatives. Rachelle relates, "I knew my dad would have no part of my marriage, so therefore no part of any children I would have. I wondered how I'd tell them, when they were old enough to understand, why their grandfather was not in my life and consequently not in theirs." Rachelle also felt anxious about how the world was going to accept her children being both black and white, and what they'd think of themselves. But Rachelle has learned a lot about merging color and backgrounds, about grace and mercy, and about creating a family identity.

The most important thing Rachelle has learned to do is to pray. And when she prays, she uses the Word of God. What does that mean? It means reading verses in prayer. "Every child is an individual and will need different things from you. As that child's personality and bent become known, God will supply. Confess God's word over them (out loud!) to guide and guard their personality. This is vital and key. Speak biblical 'truth' over them, not the 'facts' of a situation in the natural."

Rachelle's teenage children, Zach and Serah, live in a rough school district. For a time, they were enrolled in Christian

Faith School, where they flourished. But when they ran into financial difficulties, Rachelle had to register her son and daughter at the local public school.

For the first three days at the public high school, the kids tried to adjust to policemen with handcuffs and guns trying to keep the peace. They hated it. Rachelle told them, "Do not give up your faith. Don't have a bad attitude." She prayed and claimed Philippians 4:19, "And my God will meet all your needs according to his glorious riches in Christ Jesus."

> "Cast your cares on the LORD and he will sustain you; he will never let the righteous fall." (Psalms 55:22)

But Rachelle never gave up hope that God would answer her prayers and allow her kids to return to the private school. She even continued attending Christian school parent meetings.

On the third day of public school, when Rachelle went to the store, a woman from her church approached her. "I believed I'd see you," the woman began, though Rachelle had never bumped into her there before. "We didn't get to send our own children to Christian Faith," the woman continued as she pulled out her checkbook and wrote checks for the first month's tuition. That evening, when Rachelle bull-doggedly went to the Christian Faith Parent's Night, another woman approached her. "We didn't know you very well and certainly didn't want to offend you," she began apologetically, "And so when we heard about your situation, we paid for two months tuition."

That meant both kids had three months of tuition paid, amounting to thousands of dollars. The first woman ended up extending her donation another month, and in the interim Rachelle's husband received a raise and they added a new client in their home health care business. God provided. Her prayers were heard and answered. What would God do in answer to your prayers for your children? How could praying over your children give you hope?

> Let your child hear you talking to God. Not just when praying at mealtime or bedtime, but throughout the day. Driving down the road, cooking dinner, cleaning the house, walking down the street. And don't only ask for things; praise Him, thank Him.
> —Kim

What about starting the day with prayer? That's what Jesus did. "Very early in the morning, while it was still dark, Jesus got up, left the house and went off to a solitary place, where he prayed." (Mark 1:35)

1. You could begin your day by praying these words from the Old Testament:

> *Satisfy us in the morning with your unfailing love, that we may sing for joy and be glad all our days.* (Psalms 90:14)

> *In the morning, O LORD, you hear my voice; in the morning I lay my requests before you and wait in expectation.* (Psalms 5:3)

> *Let the morning bring me word of your unfailing love, for I have put my trust in you. Show me the way I should go, for to you I lift up my soul.* (Psalms 143:8)

> *Because of the LORD'S great love we are not consumed, for his compassions never fail. They are new every morning; great is your faithfulness.* (Lamentations 3:22–23)

2. You can sweeten the end of your day with prayer, too.

> *By day the LORD directs his love, at night his song is with me—a prayer to the God of my life.* (Psalms 42:8)

> *It is good to praise the LORD and make music to your name, O Most High, to proclaim your love in the morning and your faithfulness at night.* (Psalms 92:1–2)

> *I will praise the LORD, who counsels me; even at night my heart instructs me.* (Psalms 16:7)

> *My eyes stay open through the watches of the night, that I may meditate on your promises.* (Psalms 119:148)

Check out the variety of books about praying the Word over your children (listed at the end of this day's study). In

> "Arise, cry out in the night, as the watches of the night begin; pour out your heart like water in the presence of the Lord. Lift up your hands to him for the lives of your children." (Lamentations 2:19)

> "The Sovereign Lord has given me an instructed tongue, to know the word that sustains the weary. He wakens me morning by morning, wakens my ear to listen like one being taught." (Isaiah 50:4)

Stormie Omartian's *The Power of a Praying Parent*, the chapters include releasing your child to God, praying for their safety, establishing an eternal future, honoring parents, peace in their relationships, and a hunger for God. She includes plenty of topics to ignite your prayer life!

Your heartwork involves praying for your child using God's Word. In the sample prayers below, fill in the blanks with your child's name. Notice in these prayers that I've incorporated scriptures from the topics mentioned from the beginning to the end of this study. Pray a section a day, and you'll be reminded of all you've learned.

Help My Child Know Your Love

Lord, Help _____ to know You have plans for her. Plans to prosper her and not to harm her, plans to give her hope and a future. Help _____ call upon You. Listen to her. May she seek You and find You when she seeks You with all her heart. (Jeremiah 29:11–13)

May _____ understand that You are with her, You are mighty to save. You will take great delight in _____, You will quiet her with Your love, You will rejoice over her with singing. May she feel Your love and tenderness as her shepherd. May she know she is carried close to Your heart. (Zephaniah 3:17; Isaiah 40:11)

I pray that _____ being rooted and established in love, may have power, together with all the saints, to grasp how wide and long and high and deep is the love of Christ, and to know this love that surpasses knowledge—that _____ may be filled to the measure of all the fullness of God. And to be convinced that neither death nor life, neither angels nor demons, neither the present nor the future, nor any powers, neither height nor depth, nor anything else in all creation, will be able to separate us from the love of God that is in Christ Jesus our Lord. (Ephesians 3:17–19; Romans 8:38–39)

Help My Child Understand She Is Your Child

May _____ receive You and believe in Your name and be born again into the family of God. (John 1:12–13)

May _____ call You "Abba, Father" and know that she is Your child and an heir. (Galatians 4:4–7)

May _____ know Your voice and recognize that You were speaking to _____when You said, "Let the little children come to me, and do not hinder them for the kingdom of heaven belongs to such as these," You were speaking to _____. (Matthew 19:14)

Help My Child Look to You

Be her strength in times of trouble for the salvation of the righteous comes from You Lord; You are her stronghold in time of trouble. You are the Lord our God. Take hold of her right hand and say, "Do not fear; I will help you." (Psalms 37:39; Isaiah 41:13)

Help _____ understand that You are the everlasting God, the Creator, and You will not grow tired or weary but will give strength to the weary and increase the power of the weak. Help _____ to come to you, especially when she is burdened. May _____ find her rest in You. May _____ put her hope in You and renew her strength. May _____ soar on wings like eagles, run and not grow weary, walk and not be faint. (Matthew 11:28–30; Isaiah 40:28–31)

Help _____ not to fear, help her to know that You are with her, that You are her God and that You will strengthen her, help her, and uphold her with Your righteous right hand. (Isaiah 41:10)

You Lord are _____'s rock, fortress, and deliverer. May _____ take refuge in You. Be _____'s shield, salvation, and her stronghold. (Psalms 18:2)

Help _____ to set You always before her. Be at _____'s right hand so she will not be shaken. Make _____'s heart glad and her tongue rejoice. (Psalms 16:8–9)

May _____ claim, "The LORD is my light and my salvation—whom shall I fear? The LORD is the stronghold of my life—of whom shall I be afraid?" (Psalms 27:1)

Help My Child Be Still

May _____ be still, and know that You are God; You will be exalted among the nations, You will be exalted in the earth. Lead _____ beside quiet waters and restore her soul. (Psalms 37:7; 46:10; 23:2–3)

Help My Child Understand and Accept How You Made Her

May _____ praise You because she understands she is fearfully and wonderfully made; Your works are wonderful, may _____ know that full well. May she never question or doubt the potter's work but be content in how You made her. (Psalms 139:14)

Help _____ not to worry about outward appearance, or talents, or height, or weight, but to remember that You look at the heart. (1 Samuel 16:7)

I pray today that my child has faith, goodness, knowledge, self-control, perseverance, godliness, brotherly kindness, and brotherly love. And that _____ will possesses these qualities in increasing measure, knowing more and more about Jesus so she is an effective and productive Christian. (2 Peter 1:5–8)

Help My Child to Pray

Help _____ to call upon You. Answer _____, be with _____ in trouble, deliver and honor _____. (Psalms 91:15)

May _____ Cast all her anxiety on You because You caress for _____. (1 Peter 5:7)

May _____ be joyful always; pray continually. (1 Thessalonians 5:16–17)

Help My Child Ask for Forgiveness and to Forgive

Let the riches of Your kindness, tolerance, and patience lead _____ to repentance. (Romans 2:4)

May _____ have redemption through Your blood, the forgiveness of her sins in accordance with the riches of Your grace. (Ephesians 1:7)

Help _____ to confess her sins. You are faithful and just to forgive her sins and cleanse her from all unrighteousness. (1 John 1:9)

Help _____ to get rid of all bitterness, rage and anger, brawling and slander, along with every form of malice. Help her be kind and compassionate to others, forgiving others, just as You forgave her. Clothe _____ with compassion, kindness, humility, gentleness, and patience, and most of all love. (Ephesians 4:31–32; Colossians 3:12–13)

May _____ not sin in her anger. Teach her even at a young age not to let the sun go down on her anger so that the devil doesn't gain a foothold. (Ephesians 4:26–27)

May _____ throw off everything that hinders, sin that entangles, and run the race marked for _____. May _____ fix her eyes on Jesus, the author and perfecter of her faith. (Hebrews 12:1–2)

Help My Child to Serve

Help _____ not to do anything out of selfish ambition or vain conceit, but in humility consider others better than her. May she look not just to herself, but also to the interests of others. (Philippians 2:3–4)

May _____ serve wholeheartedly, as if serving the Lord, not men. (Ephesians 6:7–8)

May _____ understand that Your grace is sufficient. That when _____ is weak, then You are strong. (2 Corinthians 12:9–10)

Help My Child to Have Wise Friends

Since perfume and incense bring joy to the heart, and the pleasantness of one's friend springs from his earnest counsel, may _____ have the pleasantness of godly friends who bring joy to her heart and offer good counsel. May _____ have a good friend who loves _____ at all times and sticks close like a brother in adversity. And may my child be the kind of a friend who comforts like You have comforted us. (Proverbs 27:9; 17:17; 2 Corinthians 1:3–4)

Whatever is true, whatever is noble, whatever is right, whatever is pure, whatever is lovely, whatever is admirable—if anything is excellent or praiseworthy—help _____ think about such things. (Philippians 4:8)

Help _____ to love sincerely, hate what is evil and cling to what is good. May _____ be devoted in brotherly love and honor others. May _____ be joyful in hope, patient in affliction, and faithful in prayer. Help her to notice those in need and share with them and practice hospitality. Help _____ to bless those who persecute her, rejoice with those who rejoice, mourn with those who mourn. May _____ live in harmony with others and not to be proud, but willing to associate with people of low position. Help _____ to live at peace with others. (Romans 12)

Help My Child Hunger for Your Word

May _____ crave pure spiritual milk, so that by it _____ may grow up in her salvation. (1 Peter 2:2)

Help _____ not to conform to the world, but be transformed by renewing of her mind. Help her to be able to test and approve what Your good, pleasing and perfect will is! (Romans 12:1–2)

Help _____ not to set before her eyes any vile thing. (Psalms 101:3)

May _____ delight in You, help her to have the desires of _____ heart. May she commit her way to You and trust in You. (Psalms 37:4–5)

Help_____ not to forget Your teaching, but keep Your commands in her heart, for they will prolong her life many years and bring her prosperity. May Your words be sweet to her taste. May _____ gain understanding from your precepts and hate every wrong path. May your Word be a lamp to _____'s feet and a light to _____ path and may knowing and obeying Your law bring her peace, and keep _____ from stumbling. May she build her house on your wisdom and may she explore each room with its knowledge as if searching for rare and beautiful treasures. (Psalms 119:103–105, 165; 24:3; Proverbs 3:1–2)

Help _____ not store up treasures on earth but treasures in heaven instead. And may _____ seek first Your kingdom and Your righteousness. (Matthew 6:19–21, 33)

Help My Child Love Others

Help _____ understand that you have loved with an everlasting love and have drawn her with loving-kindness. May she walk in obedience to your commands and walk in love. (Jeremiah 31:3; 2 John 6)

Help _____ to be patient, kind, and not to envy, boast, or be proud. May she not be rude, self-seeking, easily angered or keep record of wrongs. Help _____ not to delight in evil but rejoice in the truth. Help _____'s love to protect, trust, hope, persevere, and never fail. (1 Corinthians 13)

Help My Child Rejoice in You

May _____ wake up each day with an attitude that says, "This is the day the LORD has made; let us rejoice and be glad in it." Help her to sing a new song and may her mouth be filled with laughter and be ready to proclaim what the Lord has done for _____. May _____ shout for joy to the Lord, worship Him, and come before Him with joyful songs. (Psalms 118:24; 126:2; 100:1–2)

Help My Child Trust You

Help _____ to trust in You and not to let _____'s heart be troubled. May _____ trust with all her heart and not lean on her own understanding but to acknowledge You. Make _____'s way straight. Each morning bring _____ word of Your unfailing love because _____ puts her trust in You. Show _____ the way to go as _____ lifts up her soul. May _____ be blessed because _____ trusts in You and puts her confidence in You alone. Keep _____ in perfect peace because _____ mind is steadfast and trusting in You. (John 14:1; Proverbs 3:5–6; Psalms 143:8; Jeremiah 17:7; Isaiah 26:3)

Help _____ to rejoice in suffering, and may suffering produce perseverance, then character, and then hope. (Romans 5:1–5)

Blessed is _____ who trusts in You, whose confidence is in You. May _____ be like a tree planted by the water that sends out its roots by the stream. It does not fear when heat comes; its leaves are always green. It has no worries in a year of drought and never fails to bear fruit. (Jeremiah 17:7–8)

Help _____ not to be anxious about anything, but in everything, by prayer and petition, with thanksgiving, present her requests to God. And the peace of God, which transcends all understanding, will guard _____'s heart and your mind in Christ Jesus. (Philippians 4:6–7)

Help My Child to Guard Her Heart and Mouth

May the words of _____'s mouth and the meditation of _____'s heart be pleasing in your sight, O LORD, my Rock and my Redeemer. (Psalms 19:14)

Help _____ to bear with the failings of the weak and not to please _____. Help _____ to please his neighbor for his good, and to build him up. Let _____'s conversation be always full of grace, seasoned with salt, so that _____ may know how to answer everyone. (Romans 15:1–2; Colossians 4:6)

May _____ be quick to listen, slow to speak and slow to become angry, for _____'s anger does not bring about the righteous life that You desire. (James 1:19–20)

Help My Child Look to the Light and Your Hope

Whatever happens in _____'s life, may _____ keep her lamp burning, turn _____'s darkness into light. Be _____'s light and salvation so _____ will not fear. May _____ walk in the light of your presence. Be _____'s everlasting light and glory. (Psalms 18:28; 27:1; 89:15; Isaiah 60:19)

Help My Child to Be Teachable

Help _____ not to despise your discipline, or resent your rebuke. Help my child to accept Your words, store up Your commands and turn her ear to wisdom and apply her heart to understanding. May she call out for insight and cry aloud for understanding and look for it as if for silver and search for it as for hidden treasure. May she understand the fear of the Lord and learn more of You. (Proverbs 3:11–12; 2:1–5)

May _____ recognize and proclaim, and may it be written on _____ heart that "The LORD our God, the LORD is one. Love the LORD your God with all your heart and with all your soul and with all your strength." (Deuteronomy 6:4–9)

Help _____ to obey her parents for this pleases You. (Colossians 3:20)

May _____ make every effort to keep the unity of the Spirit through the bond of peace and live in unity with _____'s brothers. (Psalms 133:1; Ephesians 4:3)

Your love is everlasting to everlasting to those who fear You. Please help _____ to fear You, keep Your covenants and remember to obey Your precepts. (Psalms 103:17–18)

Let your children know you are committed to praying for them. My friend Kim even has her prayers for her daughter Sarah posted. She encourages moms to "Pray God's gifts may be abundant to him/her. Write them down and share with your child when she is old enough. I have the prayers written and framed in her bedroom." Below are these prayers

Sarah's Gifts

GRATITUDE

May Sarah recognize all that God has given her, and daily express her gratitude to Him for all of the blessings in her life.

INCLUSIVENESS

May Sarah welcome others into any setting to which she is a part. May she display love and hospitality to all.

FELLOWSHIP

May Sarah enjoy the company of other Christians, both young and old, and learn valuable faith lessons from them.

TRUTH

May Sarah always speak the truth about others, her feelings, and situations that have occurred; even though the truth may be may be difficult for others to hear or difficult for her to say.

SPEAKING

May Sarah always be willing and able to share all that she knows about Jesus and how He has come to be a part of her life.

Sarah is certainly blessed with the gift of a praying mom!

As we close our little shower of wisdom, my friend Barb's response summed up all we learned. When asked the following question, she, like so many women, wrote about the journey.

If you were five steps ahead and could advise someone walking behind you, what would you tell them to pack for the journey of motherhood?

1. Kneepads. Without prayer, motherhood is an impossible task. The only perfect parent is God Himself, so get to know Him well.
2. A trustworthy friend who will shop with you for kneepads. A sister in Christ who is at the same point in her parenting path and is willing to love your children as her own, trade kids back and forth, and commit to spending time together in prayer for one another, husbands, and children. She will know how and what to pray for.
3. A mom further down the path with well-worn kneepads. She can give perspective, encouragement, comfort, and advice.
4. A journal to record your joys, sorrows, and for keeping a record of the ways God has worked in your family.

This journal will be a reminder of God's faithfulness and a treasure to pass onto your children.

Response: *Lord, help me get on my knees in prayer for my children. Bring a trustworthy friend alongside me who can offer perspective, encouragement, comfort, advice, and pray with me. May I always remember to praise You for your power and to thank You for how you hear my prayers. May Your righteousness continue for all generations to come as my children and I look to You in prayer and remember to obey Your precepts.* (Psalms 103:17–18)

References:

The Power of a Praying Parent, Stormie Omartian (Eugene, OR: Harvest House Publishers, 2007)

Praying the Bible for Your Children, David and Heather Kopp (Cambridge, UK: Kingsway Publications, 2002)

Watchman on the Walls, Anne Arkins and Gary Harrell (Scituate, MA: Family Life Publishing, 1995)

While They Were Sleeping: Twelve Character Traits for Moms to Pray, Gary Harrell and Anne Arkins (Family Life, 2004)

Prayers from a Mom's Heart, Fern Nichols (Grand Rapids, MI: Inspirio, 2003)

Every Child Needs a Praying Mom, Fern Nichols and Janet Kobobel Grant (Grand Rapids, MI: Zondervan, 2003)

How to Be a Praying Mom, Jeannie St. John Taylor (Peabody, MA: Hendrickson Publishers, 2001)

Praying the Scriptures for Your Children, Jodi Berndt (Grand Rapids, MI: Zondervan, 2001)

Momsintouch.org

CONCLUSION

In closing, the last chapter of Proverbs begins with King Lemuel crediting the passage to his *mother*.

"The sayings of King Lemuel—an oracle his **mother** taught him." (If a woman taught her son these words and he became king, maybe we should take note!) This chapter describes the ideal woman, then ends with praise of her and the reason for her praise. "Her children arise and call her blessed; her husband also, and he praises her: 'Many women do noble things, but you surpass them all'" (Proverbs 31:28–29).

I would love to hear my children rise up and call me blessed and to hear my husband think I'm tops among all women. And what might cause a husband and children to feel that way? Continue reading:

> *Charm is deceptive, and beauty is fleeting; but a woman who fears the LORD is to be praised. Give her the reward she has earned, and let her works bring her praise at the city gate. (Proverbs 31:30–31)*

"A woman who fears the LORD is to be praised." I hope that phrase describes you. I hope that through this study you've learned to love studying His word, and to love and trust Him. I pray you can rely on Him as you parent, and that you will teach your children all about their Lord and Savior.

In a marriage book I looked at, the author answered the question, "How would you like to be remembered by your friends and family?" Her response made me question, "How *would* I want to be remembered?" That's when I wrote this mission statement to clarify my priorities.

> *My Motherhood Mission Statement*
> *I hope my children remember me as a mom who loved and cherished them and shared the love and light of Jesus. I hope they know that my love for them is unconditional.*
> *I hope my husband feels respected, loved, honored, and that I encourage him to be the man God wants him to be.*
>
> *Ann Marie Stewart*

I hope these five weeks have prepared your heart to become the mother God wants you to become. As you leave this study, write your own mission statement of motherhood.

My Motherhood Mission Statement:

"But from everlasting to everlasting the LORD's love is with those who fear him, and his righteousness with their children's children—with those who keep his covenant and remember to obey his precepts." (Psalms 103:17–18)

I would like to end this study by offering this prayer for you,

Lord, bless this dear mom. I pray she can rely on You in her parenting and teach her children all about You and Your salvation. May she live out her mission statement and walk in Your ways, come close to You, and understand the blueprints You have for her heart. Clearly show her the priorities You have for her life, and help her to understand forgiveness and service. May she hunger for Your Word, long to spend time with You, and seek out friendships of other godly women. May she speak and listen with grace, teach her children with love, and seek wisdom from Your Word.

And now, beloved mom,

To him who is able to keep you from falling and to present you before his glorious presence without fault and with great joy—to the only God our Savior be glory, majesty, power and authority, through Jesus Christ our Lord, before all ages, now and forevermore! Amen. (Jude 24–25)

God bless your mothering. I can't wait to hear how God works in your life and the lives of your children.

Love, Ann Marie Stewart

APPENDIX

This study focused on Moms who are *into* the Word, but next you can learn about moms who are actually listed *in* the Word. This quick dash through the Bible will prompt your heart to consider what you can learn from these mothers.

Biblical Moms—Good and Bad, Named and Unnamed

*Adam named his wife **Eve**, because she would become the **mother** of all the living.* (Genesis 3:20)

That's pretty much the beginning. How would you like that title? *Mother of all the living.* In the generations of mothers that followed, some made great choices, others not so great.

Sarah wasn't sure she'd ever become a mother and even scoffed at the idea. Lacking confidence in God's plan, she offered up her handmaid to her husband. Hagar, the handmaid, had a son before Sarah gave birth, causing a schism that still reverberates through history (Genesis 16—18, 21).

We see that **Rebekah** schemed with one son, Jacob, to wrestle away his twin brother Esau's birthright (Genesis 27). Playing favorites is never a good idea.

After Jacob flees from his brother's anger, Jacob falls in love with Rachel, Laban's younger daughter. Laban tricks Jacob into marrying Rachel's older sister, Leah, before being able to marry his chosen bride, Rachel. **Rachel and Leah** started a baby boom, competing with one another for the affection of their husband Jacob (Genesis 29—31). The ensuing competition between their twelve children (the twelve tribes of Israel) set up Joseph's coat of many colors and a terrible betrayal (Genesis 37). Can you see the pattern? Mothers play a part in history, both good and bad.

We know that **Moses' mother** Jochebed saved Moses from Pharoah and the Egyptians by telling his older sister to place him in a basket in the water. This set up Pharaoh's daughter to rescue Moses and adopt him (Exodus 2).

Samson's mother lacked the backbone to strongly point out the evil of Samson's ways and thus enabled her son's poor choices (Judges 14).

> **Deborah** sang a song declaring herself a "mother in Israel."
> (Judges 5:7)

169

Hannah prayed for a baby, and God answered by giving her a son. Hannah dedicated Samuel to God and allowed Eli, the Chief Priest, to raise him in the temple. "Each year his **mother** made him a little robe and took it to him when she went up with her husband to offer the annual sacrifice" (1 Samuel 2:19).

In a fascinating story with Elisha, we see God healed the son of a **Shunammite mother** in response to her faith (2 Kings 4:8–37). But in 2 Chronicles 22:3, we also see a mother named **Athaliah** who encouraged her son to do wrong. "He too walked in the ways of the house of Ahab, for his **mother** encouraged him in doing wrong."

What a sad legacy. Still, a bad past doesn't eliminate the possibility of a fresh start. In the lineage of Christ, the prostitute **Rahab** leaves her past, marries an Israelite, and becomes a mother listed in Christ's genealogy.

Ruth, the wife of Boaz and great grandmother of King David, is also listed in the lineage. (Joshua 2; 6; Matthew 1:5; Hebrews 11: 31; James 2:35) And the mother of Solomon (who "had been **Uriah's wife**") is perhaps unnamed because she and David had committed adultery.

Their son, King Solomon, is later confronted with two mothers, one living son, and a challenging choice. When the mothers fight about who is the mother of the living son and who is the mother of the dead son, Solomon must award custody of the living son to the appropriate mother. Basically, he demands, "Will the real mom please stand up?" when he states, *"Cut the living child in two and give half to one and half to the other."* The true mother reveals herself by giving up her son to save his life. King Solomon sees her compassion and returns the baby to his rightful mother (1 Kings 3:16–28).

Moving into the New Testament, we see even **Mary, the mother of Jesus Christ,** can worry when her son is away for days. "When his parents saw him, they were astonished. His **mother** said to him, 'Son, why have you treated us like this? Your father and I have been anxiously searching for you'" (Luke 2:48). When Jesus returns in obedience with them to Nazareth, Luke 2:51 remarks, "But his **mother** treasured all these things in her heart" (emphasis added).

Many years later, when Jesus begins teaching, a woman in the crowd calls out to Him, "Blessed is the **mother** who gave you birth and nursed you." Jesus' response reveals what He believes is blessed, "Blessed rather are those who hear the word of God and obey it." (Luke 11:27–28) The importance is not on being a mother—or even being Jesus' mother, but on whether we hear Jesus' message and obey it.

Jesus healed the **children of mothers** (Matthew 15:22–28; John 9), and even raised two children from the dead right in front of their mothers (Luke 7:11–17; 8:40–56). As we studied before, Jesus reprimanded the **mother of Zebedee's sons** when she asked them to be placed on His right and left.

Later in the New Testament, Paul emphasizes the importance of certain biblical mothers and women who have been like a mother to him. "Greet Rufus, chosen in the Lord, and **his mother**, who has been a **mother** to me, too" (Romans 16:13).

In a letter to the disciple Timothy (whose father was Greek), Paul compliments the sincere faith that has been taught to Timothy by **his mother** (who from Acts 16:1 we know to be a Jewish believer) and **his grandmother.** "I have been reminded of your sincere faith, which first lived in your grandmother Lois and in your **mother** Eunice and, I am persuaded, now lives in you also" (2 Timothy 1:5).

Do you have a *sincere faith living in you*? Can you begin a legacy of faith by teaching your child, as Timothy's mother and grandmother did?

> Paul also describes the gentle way a mother cares for her children. *"As apostles of Christ we could have been a burden to you, but we were gentle among you, like a **mother** caring for her little children."* (1 Thessalonians 2:6–7)

Motherly Metaphors, Similes, and Proverbs:

And finally, throughout the Old and New Testaments, the Bible uses descriptive, maternal words to explain spiritual situations.

Ezekiel 19 describes one mother as a lioness, and another a vine.

*"What a lioness was your **mother** among the lions! She lay down among the young lions and reared her cubs."* (Ezekiel 19:2)

*"Your **mother** was like a vine in your vineyard planted by the water; it was fruitful and full of branches because of abundant water." (Ezekiel 19:10)*

To what will others compare us? How could we become a vine in a vineyard feeding on His word?

The phrase "Like mother, like daughter" is a proverb quoted in the Bible and apparently isn't always a compliment. In Ezekiel, the proverb takes an ugly shape:

*Everyone who quotes proverbs will quote this proverb about you: "Like **mother**, like daughter." You are a true daughter of your **mother**, who despised her husband and her children; and you are a true sister of your sisters, who despised their husbands and their children. Your **mother** was a Hittite and your father an Amorite. (Ezekiel 16:44–45, emphasis added)*

One New Testament mom who encouraged her daughter to do evil exemplifies "like mother, like daughter." Herodias' daughter's dance so pleased Herodias' husband, he granted his stepdaughter anything she asked, even up to half the kingdom. The stepdaughter asked her mother what she should ask for, and the mother said, "The head of John the Baptist." The Bible says, "When they returned with his head on a platter, they presented it to the girl and she gave it to her **mother**" (Mark 6:24-25, emphasis added).

Also, childbirth itself is used as a metaphor or simile throughout scripture.

Did I conceive all these people? Did I give them birth? Why do you tell me to carry them in my arms, as a nurse carries an infant, to the land you promised on oath to their forefathers? (Numbers 11:12)

You deserted the Rock, who fathered you; you forgot the God who gave you birth. (Deuteronomy 32:18)

As a woman with child and about to give birth writhes and cries out in her pain, so were we in your presence, O LORD. (Isaiah 26:17)

He chose to give us birth through the word of truth, that we might be a kind of firstfruits of all he created. (James 1:18)

Jesus even used the metaphor of birth when prophesying about His leaving and returning.

"A woman giving birth to a child has pain because her time has come; but when her baby is born she forgets the anguish because of her joy that a child is born into the world." (John 16:21)

Paul writes in Galatians 4:19–20, "My dear children, for whom I am in the pains of childbirth until Christ is formed in you, how I wish I could be with you now."

Weaning and feeding are also used as similes and metaphors. Infants need milk but as we grow stronger in our faith, we should transition from "baby food" to the solid food of His word. The following verses examine the metaphors of weaning and eating solid food (with emphasis added):

*But I have stilled and quieted my soul; like a weaned child with its **mother**, like a weaned child is my soul within me. (Psalms 131:2)*

*Brothers, I could not address you as spiritual but as worldly—mere infants in Christ. I gave you **milk**, not solid food, for you were not yet ready for it. Indeed, you are still not ready. (1 Corinthians 3:1–2)*

*In fact, though by this time you ought to be teachers, you need someone to teach you the elementary truths of God's word all over again. You need **milk**, not solid food! Anyone who lives on **milk**, being still an infant, is not acquainted with the teaching about righteousness. (Hebrews 5:12–13)*

*Like newborn babies, crave pure spiritual **milk**, so that by it you may grow up in your salvation, now that you have tasted that the Lord is good. (1 Peter 2:2–3)*

We can learn from our children and keep a childlike faith, but not remain infants in our knowledge of Him. As our children grow up in Him, may we also grow in wisdom and knowledge, speaking His truth in love.

> *Then we will no longer be infants, tossed back and forth by the waves, and blown here and there by every wind of teaching and by the cunning and craftiness of men in their deceitful scheming. Instead, speaking the truth in love, we will in all things grow up into him who is the Head, that is, Christ. (Ephesians 4:14–15)*

And finally, Proverbs offers motherly proverbs, precautions, and promises. "A wise son brings joy to his father, but a foolish son grief to his **mother**" (Proverbs 10:1; emphasis added). *May your father and **mother** be glad; may she who gave you birth rejoice!* (Proverbs 23:25; emphasis added). Many proverbs are for children, cautioning them about what happens when they do not respect their parents (Proverbs 15:20; 19:26; 20:20; 23:22; 28:24; 29:15; 30:17).

"The righteous man leads a blameless life; blessed are his children after him."
(Proverbs 20:7)

The Bible offers so much wisdom. May you find blessings by reading God's Word and applying it to your life, and may your children be blessed in your parenting.